M

Please check for 1 DVD in
BACK

D1556878

Bulldog

2nd Edition

GET MORE!
Visit www.wiley.com/
go/bulldog

Liz Palika

Howell
Book House™

This book is printed on acid-free paper.

Copyright © 2009 by Wiley Publishing, Inc., Hoboken, New Jersey. All rights reserved.

Howell Book House
Published by Wiley Publishing, Inc., Hoboken, New Jersey

No part of this publication may be reproduced, stored in a retrieval system or transmitted in any form or by any means, electronic, mechanical, photocopying, recording, scanning or otherwise, except as permitted under Sections 107 or 108 of the 1976 United States Copyright Act, without either the prior written permission of the Publisher, or authorization through payment of the appropriate per-copy fee to the Copyright Clearance Center, 222 Rosewood Drive, Danvers, MA 01923, (978) 750-8400, fax (978) 646-8600, or on the web at www.copyright.com. Requests to the Publisher for permission should be addressed to the Legal Department, Wiley Publishing, Inc., 10475 Crosspoint Blvd., Indianapolis, IN 46256, (317) 572-3447, fax (317) 572-4355, or online at http://www.wiley.com/go/permissions.

Wiley, the Wiley logo, Howell Book House, the Howell Book House logo, Your Happy Healthy Pet, and related trade dress are trademarks or registered trademarks of John Wiley & Sons, Inc. and/or its affiliates in the United States and other countries, and may not be used without written permission. All other trademarks are the property of their respective owners. Wiley Publishing, Inc. is not associated with any product or vendor mentioned in this book.

The publisher and the author make no representations or warranties with respect to the accuracy or completeness of the contents of this work and specifically disclaim all warranties, including without limitation warranties of fitness for a particular purpose. No warranty may be created or extended by sales or promotional materials. The advice and strategies contained herein may not be suitable for every situation. This work is sold with the understanding that the publisher is not engaged in rendering legal, accounting, or other professional services. If professional assistance is required, the services of a competent professional person should be sought. Neither the publisher nor the author shall be liable for damages arising here from. The fact that an organization or Website is referred to in this work as a citation and/or a potential source of further information does not mean that the author or the publisher endorses the information the organization or Website may provide or recommendations it may make. Further, readers should be aware that Internet Websites listed in this work may have changed or disappeared between when this work was written and when it is read.

For general information on our other products and services or to obtain technical support please contact our Customer Care Department within the U.S. at (800) 762-2974, outside the U.S. at (317) 572-3993 or fax (317) 572-4002.

Wiley also publishes its books in a variety of electronic formats. Some content that appears in print may not be available in electronic books. For more information about Wiley products, please visit our web site at www.wiley.com.

Library of Congress Cataloging-in-Publication Data:
Library of Congress Cataloging-in-Publication data is available from the publisher upon request.

ISBN: 978-0-470-39054-2

Printed in the United States of America

10 9 8 7 6 5 4 3 2 1

2nd Edition

Book design by Melissa Auciello-Brogan
Cover design by Michael J. Freeland
Book production by Wiley Publishing, Inc. Composition Services

About the Author

Liz Palika has been teaching dogs and their owners in Northern San Diego County for almost twenty-five years. Her training is based on an understanding of dogs and what makes them tick. There is no funny stuff but lots of common sense.

Liz is also the author of more than fifty books; her dog training book *All Dogs Need Some Training* was listed by *Pet Life* magazine as one of the ten best dog training books available to dog owners. Liz's books have been honored with several awards from Dog Writers Association of America, Cat Writers' Association, ASPCA, Purina, and San Diego Book Writers. Liz was honored by San Diego Channel 10's Leadership Award; she was also a North County Woman of Merit. In 2005, she was awarded a Distinguished Service award from Dog Writers Association of America.

Liz is a charter member of the International Association of Canine Professionals, and is a Certified Dog Trainer (CDT) through this organization. She is also a member of the International Association of Animal Behavior Consultants, and an AKC CGC (Canine Good Citizen) Evaluator.

About Howell Book House

Since 1961, Howell Book House has been America's premier publisher of pet books. We're dedicated to companion animals and the people who love them, and our books reflect that commitment. Our stable of authors—training experts, veterinarians, breeders, and other authorities—is second to none. And we've won more Maxwell Awards from the Dog Writers Association of America than any other publisher.

As we head toward the half-century mark, we're more committed than ever to providing new and innovative books, along with the classics our readers have grown to love. From bringing home a new puppy to competing in advanced equestrian events, Howell has the titles that keep animal lovers coming back again and again.

Contents

Shopping List

You'll need to do a bit of stocking up before you bring your new dog or puppy home. Below is a basic list of some must-have supplies. For more detailed information on the selection of each item below, consult chapter 5. For specific guidance on what grooming tools you'll need, review chapter 7.

☐ Food dish (a shallow one to accommodate the Bulldog's short muzzle)

☐ Water dish

☐ Dog food

☐ Leash

☐ Collar

☐ ID tag

☐ Crate (make it metal wire, because a Bulldog may chew through a plastic or soft-sided one)

☐ Nail clippers

☐ Grooming tools

☐ Toys

☐ Chew toys (heavy duty for power chewers)

There are likely to be a few other items that you're dying to pick up before bringing your dog home. Use the following blanks to note any additional items you'll be shopping for.

☐ _____

☐ _____

☐ _____

☐ _____

☐ _____

☐ _____

☐ _____

☐ _____

☐ _____

☐ _____

Pet Sitter's Guide

We can be reached at (___)_____-_____ Cell phone (___)_____-_____

We will return on _____ (date) at _____ (approximate time)

Dog's Name _____

Breed, Age, and Sex _____

Important Names and Numbers

Vet's Name _____ Phone (___)_____- _____

Address_____

Emergency Vet's Name _____ Phone (___)_____- _____

Address_____

Poison Control _____ (or call vet first)

Other individual (someone the dog knows well and will respond to) to contact in case of emergency or in case the dog is being protective and will not allow the pet sitter in _____

Care Instructions

In the following three blanks let the sitter know what to feed, how much, and when; when the dog should go out; when to give treats; and when to exercise the dog.

Morning_____

Afternoon_____

Evening _____

Medications needed (dosage and schedule) _____

Any special medical conditions _____

Grooming instructions _____

My dog's favorite playtime activities, quirks, and other tips_____

Part I
The World of the Bulldog

The Bulldog

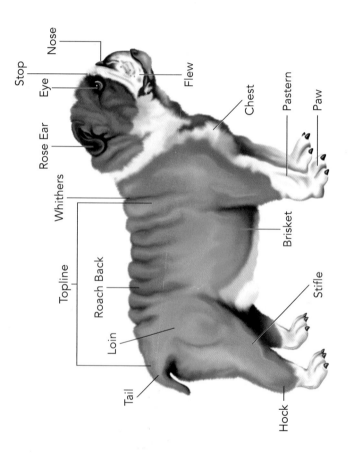

Nose
Stop
Eye
Flew
Rose Ear
Chest
Pastern
Paw
Whithers
Topline
Brisket
Roach Back
Loin
Stifle
Tail
Hock

Chapter 1

What Is a Bulldog?

One of the most popular mascots for colleges, universities, and sporting teams in the world is the Bulldog. Georgetown University in Washington, D.C., and California State University, Fresno, both have Bulldog mascots, as does the University of North Carolina in Asheville. James Madison University's Bulldog mascot is called the Duke Dog, Mississippi State University's Bulldog is Bully, and the University of Puerto Rico's mascot is Tarzan.

Bulldogs are also popular with sporting teams. Great Britain's Rugby League has a team called the Batley Bulldogs. In South Africa, another rugby team is called the Border Bulldogs, and in Denmark, an ice hockey team is called the Odense Bulldogs.

The most popular Bulldog mascot of all has to be the U.S. Marine Corps' Chesty. During World War I, the Germans called the U.S. Marines *teufel-hunden*, which means "devil dogs." *Teufel-hunden* were fictitious ferocious dogs of German folklore. The Marines, of course, took this as a compliment. The first Bulldog to serve as a U.S. Marines mascot was Pvt. Jiggs in 1922, and he has been followed by numerous other Bulldogs—all serving in the image of the *teufel-hunden*.

Why are Bulldogs so popular as mascots? They are tenacious and single-minded; they are courageous and fearless; and they are devoted and loyal. All of these characteristics are admired by sports competitors, fans, and warriors alike.

Although a Bulldog is a symbol of tenacity, courage, and strength, he is also more than that. If given half a chance, he will be one of the best friends you will ever have. He accepts you as you are, whether you are a success or a failure, happy or sad, lazy or energetic, young or old.

English or American?

The Bulldog discussed in this book is the breed that is called simply *Bulldog*. Years ago, when the breed originated in Great Britain, it was known as the English Bulldog. Although many enthusiasts still call the short, stocky dogs by this name, the breed's correct name as it is recognized by the American Kennel Club is simply Bulldog.

The American Bulldog is a completely different breed. Although the American Bulldog has a shared British heritage with the original Bulldog, today it is a taller, longer-legged dog who looks little like the Bulldog of today. This breed developed in the American colonies with early settlers and was used as a hunting dog, herding dog, and companion.

The dogs now known as Old English Bulldogge are yet another breed that shares a heritage with the English Bulldog. Enthusiasts have tried to re-create the Bulldogs of yesteryear—a short, stocky dog with a wide chest—but without the exaggerated features of the Bulldog of today.

All of these breeds have their own unique characteristics, and people enjoy them for what they are. However, in this book, we're talking about the Bulldog who is called just that: the Bulldog.

The Bulldog's Physical Appearance

The Bulldog has a very unique appearance—so unique that there are very few people who would not instantly recognize a Bulldog. Let's take a look at this breed and see what makes it so different from other breeds. This physical description is based on the breed standard (see the box on page 15).

Appearance and Attitude

The perfect Bulldog must be medium size with a heavy, thick-set, low-slung body, a massive short-faced head, wide shoulders, and strong legs. The general appearance and attitude should suggest great strength, stability of temperament, and the ability to get the job done. Most males will be in the 55- to 65-pound range, and females will be in the 45- to 50-pound range.

The Bulldog is a decorous, self-respecting, confident animal. He does not pick fights, but if attacked, he will defend himself and protect the people he cares about. In the absence of his owner, the Bulldog might invite an intruder in, show him around, and then lead him to the silverware. Because the Bulldog's general appearance belies his demeanor, the intruder may not accept the invitation and the silverware will likely remain safe.

In the beginning, Bulldogs were bred for bull-baiting and fighting (more on that in chapter 2). If the dog was to survive, he therefore had to be lean, agile, and athletic. When this inhumane, vicious sport was outlawed, the purpose of the dog changed and so did his appearance and temperament. He became shorter, chunkier, a companion, a gentle and loving friend, and something of a couch potato.

The Head

The Bulldog, of course, has a very distinctive head. His skull is quite large. So large, in fact, that the circumference of the skull in front of the ears should measure at least as much as the height of the dog at the shoulders. The cheeks are well rounded and bulge sideways past the eyes. There is an indentation between the eyes, dividing the head vertically.

The eyes should be placed at the point where the forehead and the cheeks meet. They are round and very dark. If the eyes of humans are windows to our souls, the eyes of the Bulldog are certainly windows to his personality; they portray kindness, gentleness, and interest. They should be alert but not looking for trouble.

The Bulldog's expression depends greatly on the proper shape and carriage of the ears. The ears should be set high on the head and wide apart. They should be

The Bulldog's head and face are his most distinguishing features.

The Bulldog's body is short, strong, and muscular. The topline dips a bit, with the lowest point at the tops of the shoulders.

small and thin. The shape known as rose ear is considered the most desirable. The rose ear folds over and back, revealing the inside of the burr. Erect ears and button ears (where the ear flaps fold forward) are considered undesirable.

The face is short, with a broad, short muzzle that is turned upward. The nose is large, broad, and black, and the tip is set deeply between the eyes. Historically, this placement of the nose enabled the dog to breathe as he hung onto the bull. In addition, the wrinkle pattern on the face prevented any blood from getting into his nose.

The jaws should be massive, broad, square, and undershot—the lower jaw projects considerably in front of the upper jaw and turns up. This undershot bite makes it possible for the dog to hang on almost indefinitely.

The Body

The Bulldog's chest is broad, and the front legs are short, muscular, and set wide apart. The calves of the legs are well developed. Because of this, the dog appears bow-legged, but the bones of the legs should not be curved. The body should be very capacious, with full sides and well-rounded ribs. It should be very deep from the shoulders down to its lowest part where it joins the chest, giving the dog a broad, low, short-legged appearance.

The back should be short and strong, very broad at the shoulders and comparatively narrow at the loins (the area just behind the ribs). The hind legs should be

What Is a Breed Standard?

A breed standard is a detailed description of the perfect dog of that breed. Breeders use the standard as a guide in their breeding programs, and judges use it to evaluate the dogs in conformation shows. The standard is written by the national breed club, using guidelines established by the registry that recognizes the breed (such as the AKC or UKC).

Usually, the first section of the breed standard gives a brief overview of the breed's history. Then it describes the dog's general appearance and size as an adult. Next is a detailed description of the head and neck, then the back and body, and the front and rear legs. The standard then describes the ideal coat and how the dog should be presented in the show ring. It also lists all acceptable colors, patterns, and markings. Then there's a section on how the dog moves, called *gait*. Finally, there's a general description of the dog's temperament.

Each section also lists characteristics that are considered to be faults or disqualifications in the conformation ring. Superficial faults in appearance are often what distinguish a pet-quality dog from a show- or competition-quality dog. However, some faults affect the way a dog moves or his overall health. And faults in temperament are serious business.

You can read all the AKC breed standards at www.akc.org.

strong and muscular and longer than the forelegs, to elevate the loins above the shoulders. Along the topline, there should be a slight fall in the back, with the lowest point close behind the shoulders. From there, the spine should rise to the loins, then curve again more suddenly to the tail. This forms an arch, which is a very distinctive feature of the breed. This topline is called a roach back or wheel back.

The tail may be either straight or screwed, but never curved or curly. It is short and hung low on the back, with a thick root and a fine tip. The dog carries it down. The tail is never docked. It may appear too long at birth, but puppies grow faster than their tails.

Skin

It almost seems like the Bulldog has more skin than he needs. Puppies, especially, seem to be able to turn around inside their skin. The skin on both puppies and adults is soft and loose, especially at the head, neck, and shoulders. His head and face are covered with wrinkles. At the throat, from jaw to chest, there should be two loose pendulous folds. These form the dewlap.

Coat and Color

The coat is short, smooth, and fine. The preferred colors are red brindle, any other brindle, solid white, solid red, or fawn (brindle is a color pattern in which black alternates with another color to produce a striped effect). Piebald (a pattern with comparatively large patches of two or more colors, one of which is usually white) is also allowed. Only solid black is considered objectionable in the breed standard. But, like beauty, the preferred color is really in the eyes of the beholder. And Bulldogs can be found in many different colors and shades of color.

Gait

The Bulldog has a unique way of moving with a loose-jointed, shuffling, sidewise motion giving the breed its characteristic roll. This distinctive gait is the

Bulldog puppies seem to have way more skin than they need.

result of the dog's heavy, wide shoulders, short front legs with longer hind legs, and narrow rear. In spite of all this, the Bulldog can move quickly and jump a reasonable height (such as up on your bed, or into the back of the van when it's time to go somewhere).

The Bulldog's Character

Bulldogs, especially Bulldog puppies, can be silly creatures. With a perpetual smile on their faces, Bulldogs love to have fun. And when their owners laugh, Bulldogs get even sillier, wiggling the back half of their body, walking sideways, and panting with joy. But Bulldogs are also devoted, dedicated companions who know no fear and will protect their people at all costs.

Friends and Companions

The Bulldog today is first and foremost a companion. This is not a dog to be left in the backyard for hours at a time. Rather, he deserves a spot on the floor at your feet, or better yet, a place on the sofa right next to you.

Bulldogs are loyal, affectionate companions who will greet you with a smiling face and wiggling body each time you come home—and it doesn't matter whether you've been gone five minutes or five hours. Bulldogs are great family dogs, and although puppies can be clumsy and rowdy, the breed is known to be very patient with children.

Trainability

Bulldogs have a reputation for being difficult to train. This usually comes about because the owner or trainer tried to use very forceful or rough training techniques. Bulldogs have a very well-developed sense of what is fair, and rough training techniques will cause the dog to rebel or stop trying. If you try to gain the dog's cooperation instead and find out what motivates the dog (food rewards, toys, verbal praise, or a play session), you'll find out that Bulldogs are very trainable.

Many Bulldogs have competed successfully in many dog sports, including competitive obedience, agility, and flyball. Bulldogs have also served as wonderful therapy dogs.

If Bulldogs have a weakness, it is that they are not always as willing to please their owners as they are to please themselves. Bulldogs know what they want—comfort, a chance to snooze in the sunshine, food, or a favorite toy. Repeating obedience commands or exercises isn't always on the Bulldog's list of favorite

Although they have a reputation for being tough to train, if you work with what motivates your dog, you can gain his cooperation.

things to do. So it's the wise owner who learns how to motivate their Bulldog so they can gain his cooperation.

Bulldog Mythology

There are many myths about Bulldogs. Some may have a basis in reality, while others do not. Many are rooted in the Bulldog's original occupation as a fighting dog. Let's take a look at some of the most common myths.

Bulldogs Are Dangerous Around Livestock

This originated from the breed's ancestral job of fighting bulls and other large animals. As you will read in chapter 2, the breed was used for blood sports, but that was many years ago. Bulldogs today have no desire to attack larger animals. Most Bulldogs have probably never even seen a bull, and if they did, would have no idea what to do with it!

That said, if a large animal were to charge you while your Bulldog was with you, your dog would not back down from the challenge. Unfortunately, your Bulldog might get hurt in the process, because the breed we know today as a Bulldog is very different from the dogs who were used for fighting many years ago. So try not to put your Bulldog in a position where he might be faced with such a situation.

Bulldogs Fight Other Dogs

During the era of the blood sports, dogs were used to fight many other animals, including other dogs. Dogfighting became even more popular when blood sports were made illegal and the fighting went underground. Today's Bulldog, however, is mellow and calm compared to those dogs of yesteryear. Bulldogs are usually more interested in playing than squabbling.

Bulldogs are very strong for their size, though, and can be quite physical. Many dogs of other breeds play much differently and may not like the way Bulldogs play. This can lead to disagreements—growling, raised hackles, and even dogfights. Even though a Bulldog will rarely begin a fight, if one is brought to him, he won't back down.

Bulldogs Are Not Safe Around Children

As with the previous two myths, this probably originates with the breed's history. And although Bulldogs are great with kids, the sad fact is that many children are hurt or killed by dogs every year. Dogs of all breeds, even small breeds, have bitten children in a variety of situations.

Bulldogs are very patient and gentle with kids.

It's important that parents teach their children the rules of interacting with dogs safely and teach their dogs to be calm and gentle with the kids. In addition, dogs and children should never be left alone together without parental supervision.

This said, Bulldogs are great with kids. They tolerate play that many other dogs will protest, and they are incredibly patient with kids' games. Numerous Bulldogs have been dressed in baby clothes, complete with frilly hats that look so wrong above that Bulldog face!

When dogs and children both are taught the rules for correct behavior with each other, Bulldogs can be great family pets.

Chapter 2

The Bulldog Yesterday and Today

Authorities differ so completely about the origin of the Bulldog that the name itself is in dispute. While some believe the breed derives its name from the bull-like shape of the head, others maintain that the name came from the ancient custom of using Bulldogs in the sport of bull-baiting. There appears to be little doubt, however, that an early canine species resembling the Bulldog has been in existence for centuries.

Some early references indicate that the oldest English spelling of the name was probably *Bondogge* or *Bolddogge*. Later, the *Bandogge* was mentioned by William Shakespeare (1564–1616) in act 1, scene 4 of *The Second Part of Henry VI*. Conjurer Roger Bolingbrook describes the time when wizards do their work as "The time of night when Troy was set on fire; The time when screech-owls cry, and bandogges howl; And spirits walk, and ghosts break up their graves. . . ."

Possibly the first use of the modern spelling is found in a letter from 1631, written to George Willingham of St. Swithins Lane, London, from Prestwick Eaton of St. Sabastian, requesting "two good mastiffs and two good bulldogs." That letter seems to establish that Bulldogs and Mastiffs were two distinct breeds of dogs in Britain.

Origins of the Breed

Both the Bulldog and the Mastiff are believed to have a common origin in the extinct breed known as the *Alaunt* (also written *Alaune* or *Allan*). In "The

The large head and jaws of the Bulldog were originally developed to help her hold on during fights with other animals.

Knight's Tale," published in 1390, Geoffrey Chaucer described the Alaunt as a white dog "as large as any steer" and having great strength and courage. The breed was used for chasing lions and bears.

Randle Cotgrave's *A Dictionarie of the French and English Tongues*, published in London in 1611, says the Allan de Bouchere, "is like our Mastiff" and is used "to bring in fierce oxen, and to keepe their stalls." In the descriptions of these dogs, there are three distinct Bulldog characteristics that remain to this day: large, thick heads; short muzzles; and fierce courage. When attacked, they hung onto their opponent by their teeth. Bandogges or Bulldogs also were known to have been crossbred with various other breeds to correct the other breeds' lack of courage, tenacity, and determination.

Early Bulldogs were heavier than they are today, although they have always maintained an exceptional degree of tenacity and stamina. The early Bulldogs were also quite powerful, ferocious animals. In temperament, they were not the soft-hearted, friendly companions of the modern era.

Bull-Baiting

There can be no doubt that the Bulldog was originally bred for bull- and bear-baiting, as well as for fighting other dogs. These "baits" were held in roped-off enclosures, and the object was to see whether the dog could approach a tethered bull or bear, grab him, and pin him to the ground. The enraged animal would attempt to dislodge the dog, and terrible injuries to both often resulted. Spectators lost and won large sums based on the outcome of such contests.

At that time, the Bulldog was quite large, weighing from 80 to 100 pounds or more. The sport of bull-baiting was popular with all classes of British society in the 1500s and 1600s, particularly around London and the Midlands. There were bullrings and dog pits in many areas. In the beginning, the dog would attack the bull by the ear and hang on until the bull was exhausted. Later, the bull's nose was the target, and a smaller, quicker dog was more efficient.

The inhumane practice of bull-baiting was finally outlawed in Great Britain in 1835. Although there were still illegal dogfights, Bulldog breeding soon diminished, since the dogs apparently no longer served a useful purpose. Had it not been for a handful of Englishmen who saw the virtue of preserving this exceptional breed, the banning of bull-baiting would have resulted in the extinction of the Bulldog.

The Evolving Bulldog

Selective breeding brought into being the Bulldog of today, who is as loving and loyal as her predecessors were vicious. Among those who saved and transformed the breed was William George, who devoted himself to securing a more honorable status for Bulldogs. Breaking away from the low and cruel practice of dog-fighting, he gave his kennel the lofty name of Canine Castle. There he produced several outstanding dogs. One of them was Young King Dick, who was reputed to be a remarkable specimen of that era.

Recent research reveals that the first known written description of the breed was produced in 1860 on a parchment scroll in Britain. The first class for Bulldogs at a dog show was at Birmingham, also in 1860.

Selective breeding changed the Bulldog from a tough but vicious dog to a loyal and loving dog.

Bulldog Clubs

The first Bulldog club, simply named the Bulldog Club, was organized in Britain on November 3, 1864. The club had thirty members, and their motto was "Hold Fast." Their stated objective was "the perpetuation and the improvement of the old English bulldog."

The Bulldog Club's major accomplishment during the three years it existed was drafting in 1865 the first official Bulldog breed standard. It was written by the club's treasurer, Samuel Wickens, and was referred to as the Philo-Kuon standard—which was actually the author's pen name.

For the next ten years, the number of Bulldogs entered at dog shows began to increase, and classes for dogs and bitches were offered in various weight categories from 12 pounds to 25 pounds and over. However, it was not long before Spanish Bulldogs—some weighing as much as 100 pounds—were imported into Britain. The British breeders believed these dogs could threaten the continuation of the purebred English Bulldog.

In March 1875, a group of British breeders met and reconstituted the former Bulldog Club at a London pub called the Blue Post. (The pub still exists today at Newman and Oxford Streets, but has been renamed the Rose and Crown.) At this time, a written standard of perfection for the breed, describing the complete anatomy of the Bulldog, was formulated; it was published on May 27, 1875. A table of points for the standard was adopted by the club and published on September 2, 1875.

Bulldogs in North America

The first Bulldog to be exhibited at a dog show in North America was a dog named Donald, who was whelped in 1875. He was shown at New York in 1880 by Sir William Verner. Donald was brindle and white and reportedly weighed about 40 pounds.

The Bulldog breed standard hasn't changed much since 1896.

The first Bulldog was registered with the American Kennel Club in 1886. He was a brindle and white dog named Bob, sired by Taurus ex Millie and owned by Thomas Patten of Appleton, Wisconsin.

In 1888, a British-bred Bulldog named Robinson Crusoe became the first AKC Bulldog champion. In 1896, the first American-bred AKC champion was Rodney L Ambassadeur, a male owned and bred by Charles Hopton. Hopton was a successful breeder on both sides of the Atlantic, and his Rodney kennel name was said to denote both quality and soundness in the breed. The first American-bred Bulldog bitch to attain her AKC championship was Princess Merlow, owned by Harry Ruston.

Developing an American Standard

Americans used the British breed standard until a committee was formed in 1894 to modify it. The club officially adopted what was believed to be a more informative, concisely worded standard in 1896.

Since then, the American conformation standard has remained almost entirely intact. There have been only two revisions, and both times they concerned the dog's nose. On September 5, 1914, the description of the "butterfly or parti-colored" nose as highly undesirable was deleted, and instead, the "dudley or flesh-colored" nose was made the breed's only disqualifying fault. The latest revision, on July 20, 1976, deleted "dudley or flesh-colored nose" and substituted "brown or liver-colored nose" as the disqualifying fault.

The Bulldog Club of America

English Bulldogs were being imported, bred, and shown in the United States about ten years before H. D. Kendall, a breeder from Lowell, Massachusetts,

What Is the AKC?

The American Kennel Club (AKC) is the oldest and largest pure-bred dog registry in the United States. Its main function is to record the pedigrees of dogs of the breeds it recognizes. While AKC registration papers are a guarantee that a dog is pure-bred, they are absolutely not a guarantee of the quality of the dog—as the AKC itself will tell you.

The AKC makes the rules for all the canine sporting events it sanctions and approves judges for those events. It is also involved in various public education programs and legislative efforts regarding dog ownership. The AKC has also helped establish a foundation to study canine health issues and a program to register microchip numbers for companion animal owners. The AKC has no individual members—its members are national and local breed clubs and clubs dedicated to various competitive sports.

conceived the idea of forming a Bulldog club in the United States. The objective of the organization was "to join together for the purpose of encouraging the thoughtful and careful breeding of the English Bulldog in America, to perpetuate the purity of the strain, to improve the quality of native stock, and to remove the undesirable prejudice that existed in the public mind against a most admirable breed."

With those goals, the Bulldog Club of America (BCA) was formed by a group of eight interested fanciers at a New England Kennel Club all-breed dog show in Boston on April 1, 1890. The club was

The Bulldog Club of America is one of the oldest active breed clubs in the United States.

The Bulldog has always been known for her photogenic good looks.

incorporated in New York State on February 29, 1904. The Bulldog Club of America is one of the oldest active purebred dog clubs in the United States.

The Bulldog Today

The breeders and fanciers of the Bulldog have taken part in a remarkable process of evolution. Although it has taken many, many years, a snarling, fighting, aggressive animal has been changed into a gentle, quiet companion. Bulldogs have gone from bull-baiting arenas and fighting rings to becoming the beloved mascots of football teams. Many colleges have the Bulldog as their sports mascot because of the Bulldog's history of giving her all to be the winner. Today we expect to see the Yale Bulldog or the Butler Bulldog sitting on the team bench. Many high schools throughout the nation also have Bulldog mascots, hoping that the Bulldog tenacity will somehow rub off on their team.

Advertisers are using the Bulldog more and more to attract public attention to their products. Mack trucks were long represented by a Bulldog. The term *Bulldog grip* is often used to describe the hold of various tools, especially wrenches and pliers. The Bulldog's appearance is unique, and she gives a good account of herself before the camera.

The Bulldog who played Lucky Dog entertained us at dog shows as he toted his Purina dog food. Many of us enjoyed the television series *Jake and the Fatman* because we always anxiously awaited the appearance of Max (actually, Ch. Breckley Buford Win and Grin). In addition to his skills as an entertainer, this dog won his AKC championship and Companion Dog obedience title all in one year. He brought honor to the breed and joy to his owners.

How Popularity Harms

Bulldog breeders and owners have a sincere interest in protecting the breed from overbreeding. To some extent, the Bulldog herself provides some protection against that happening, because Bulldogs are not prolific breeders. Their litters are small when compared with many other breeds, and cesarean sections are almost always necessary, so the initial cost of breeding is greater than with most other breeds.

Famous Bulldog Owners

Ed Asner

Truman Capote

George Clooney

Calvin Coolidge

Warren G. Harding

Olivia de Havilland

Ice-T

Stan Lee

Nancy Milford

Vincent Price

Adam Sandler

Howard Stern

Tennessee Williams

Woodrow Wilson

When a breed is too popular, not every breeder makes a serious commitment to the well-being of the breed. Too many puppies can mean not enough good homes.

Bulldog breeders recognize that there are too many puppies being born (of all breeds) each year who will become homeless and die untimely deaths. Breeders do not want this fate for Bulldogs (or any dog), so, under the direction of BCA, a Bulldog rescue group was established. Humane societies and animal shelters know whom to call in their area if a Bulldog is brought to them; veterinarians also know whom to call if they receive an unwanted Bulldog. At the expense of BCA, this homeless, unwanted animal is given a complete physical examination, medical care, and neutering, and will soon be ready for a new home that has been evaluated for suitability. For a reasonable sum, the new owner has a wonderful Bulldog. The dog is to be returned to rescue if for some reason she can no longer stay in her new home. Many other breed clubs have established the same type of rescue program.

Breeding dogs and owning dogs are serious, long-term commitments. It has been said that the measure of a man can be taken by the way he treats children and dogs!

Breed-Specific Legislation

Unfortunately, the Bulldog's appearance, popularity (in numbers), and ancient occupation have often lead to trouble. The breed's unique face is often seen as aggressive rather than comical, and people are afraid of her.

There have also been Bulldogs who have bitten people. Poorly bred, unsocialized, abused or neglected, untrained Bulldogs can be a threat to anyone within reach. These dogs may bite out of frustration with their lot in life, or they may bite because they are afraid. Unfortunately, any bite by a Bulldog reflects badly on the breed as a whole.

What Is BSL?

Breed-specific legislation (or, as it is commonly known, BSL) is any law that limits or forbids the ownership of certain kinds or dogs. Although Pit Bull-type dogs have been the primary target, Bulldogs have also been the focus of many breed-specific laws. These laws are usually introduced after a bad biting incident in a community. Perhaps a dog ran out the front door and chased down some kids running past, and when she caught the kids, she bit one of them. City or community lawmakers and parents hate incidents like these (so do dog owners!) and strive to prevent any more of them.

Unfortunately, BSL is not fair. An entire breed should never be punished because one or a few dogs have caused a problem.

There Are Better Ways

Another problem with BSL is that it doesn't work. Many communities that have passed BSL laws have found that the incidence of dog bites has increased rather than decreased. This is usually because the legislation focused on a few breeds rather than on problem dogs and problem owners.

Wiser communities have instituted other programs to counter dog bite problems.

Breed-specific legislation can make it difficult for us to have the breed of dog we love.

- Dog clubs, dog trainers, veterinarians, humane societies, and shelters can emphasize responsible dog ownership. Flyers, brochures, classes, and newspaper articles can help dog owners learn more about their dogs and how to train and care for them correctly.
- Dog bite prevention programs in day care centers and schools have been very successful. Many dog clubs offer these programs, and the AKC has a free education program for elementary school children.
- Instead of blaming a breed of dog for a problem, the owner should be held responsible for the actions of his dog—or the owner's lack of action in confining, controlling, training, and socializing his dog.

All dog owners need to be involved in their community. Legislation that threatens to erode dog owners' rights to keep a dog are dangerous. Know what's going on in your city, county, and state, and stay involved.

Chapter 3

The World According to Bulldogs

Today's Bulldogs make wonderful pets. After many years of careful breeding, all of the Bulldog's excellent qualities have been retained and the fighting temperament has been bred out.

While we were in the U.S. Marine Corps, my husband, Paul, and I cared for and trained one of the Marine Corps' mascots named Chesty. We were assigned to Marine Barracks "8th & I" in Washington, D.C., and Chesty went to work with us every day and came home with us at night. He played with our two German Shepherd Dogs and had no idea his legs weren't as long as theirs; he sure tried hard enough to keep up! Chesty played hard, trained hard, slept hard, and ate, well, you know.

Every Bulldog is unique, but they all share many of the same characteristics. First and foremost is a courageous personality. Second is a distinctive appearance. And third is a devotion to their people.

Are You Ready for a Dog?

Adding a dog to your household should be a well-thought-out decision. You will be taking on the responsibility of a living, thinking, caring animal who will give you his heart. That's a big responsibility.

A dog should never be acquired as an impulse. It's always best to think through what is involved in owning a dog and be honest with yourself. So let's take a look at dog ownership and see if you can do what is needed for any dog, and then we'll look specifically at Bulldogs.

- Do you have time for a dog? Dogs need your time for companionship, affection, play, and training. You cannot dash in the door, toss down some dog food, and leave again. That's not fair, and the dog will react badly to it.
- Do you live in a place where dogs are allowed and welcome? If you rent your home, do you have permission from your landlord to have a dog? Not all neighborhoods are dog friendly, so make sure a dog will be welcome before you bring one home.
- Who, besides yourself, will be living with the dog? Is everyone in agreement to get a dog? If you want the dog but someone else in the household is afraid or doesn't like the dog, the situation could become very difficult.
- Is there someone in the family who could have a hard time with the dog? Is there a baby in the house, someone who is very frail, or a senior citizen with poor balance? Dogs can be unaware of their strength and size, especially when they're puppies.
- Do you have other pets in the household? Will your cat enjoy having a dog in the house? You may have to protect your rabbit, ferret, or gerbil from a rambunctious puppy.
- Have you lived with a dog before? Do you know what to expect? Really? Dogs can shed, drag in dirt and leaves from outside, catch and kill a rodent and then throw up the remains on the living room sofa.
- Do you have the money to care for a dog? Dogs need to be spayed or neutered, need vaccinations, and may hurt themselves, requiring emergency veterinary care. They'll need regular vet checkups, too. Plus, you will need a dog crate, leash and collar, toys, and dog food.

Dog ownership is wonderful. Dogs are the ultimate confidant and never reveal your secrets. They are security in a scary world and the best friend a person could have— but only if you are really ready for the responsibilities of caring for one.

It's a lot of work and a lifetime commitment to take care of a dog. Make sure everyone in your family is ready.

The Pet Bulldog

Bulldogs are people dogs. Unlike other breeds, which might be happy outside sniffing out rodents or flushing birds in the backyard, Bulldogs need to be inside with their people. A Bulldog left outside for many hours a day will be very unhappy. This could cause barking that will annoy your neighbors or destructive chewing that could destroy your wooden deck, the lawn furniture, or anything else in the backyard. Unhappy Bulldogs have also been known to be self-destructive, chewing or licking on a paw until they create a sore that will not heal.

A happy Bulldog, however, is unmistakable. His smile, wiggling body, and twitching tail will tell you exactly how much he loves you!

Bulldog Characteristics

Tenacious

Loyal

Loving

Good with kids

Dislikes rain

Likes routine

Thrives on attention

Kids and Bulldogs

Bulldogs seem to understand that babies and little children are special and need special treatment. He will tolerate their poking and prodding, and if a child gets

Your Bulldog is not a backyard kind of dog. He needs to live inside with you.

too rough, the dog will simply leave. However, in all fairness to the dog and for the safety of children, they should not be left alone together. Small children and puppies are not a good combination, simply because Bulldog puppies are big, clumsy, and often have little self-control.

Some people believe a puppy and a baby must grow up together if the puppy is to accept the child. This is not necessarily true. Some toddlers think puppies are toys. They like to poke at the puppy's eyes or pull at his ears or maybe use the puppy to sit on. The puppy might think the toddler is something to chew. When the pup tries to defend himself by biting, he is reprimanded, although he has really only protected himself from the curious toddler.

Bulldogs Like Routine

If you take your Bulldog for a daily morning walk, he will come to expect it and may even bring his leash to you. (Unless it's raining; most Bulldogs do not like to walk in the rain or through puddles after a rain.) Your Bulldog will also learn when to expect his meals, when to go to bed, and even when to expect you home from work.

Bulldogs are very much creatures of habit. Although this can help in some respects—housetraining is much easier on a schedule—it can have some unexpected consequences. If the schedule changes, your Bulldog may be unhappy. Say, for example, you are due home from work at 5:30 but decide to stop off to visit a friend. Your Bulldog will be waiting for you to come home, and when you don't show up on time, he may begin to bark, or he may have a housetraining accident.

Introducing New Things

Sometimes a Bulldog's need for routine can cause problems beyond a time schedule. New furniture may be chewed on simply because it's new and different. New dogs in the household may not be allowed inside or a new cat may be chased.

Anything new needs to be introduced to the Bulldog. With the dog on a leash, walk him up to the new item (or pet) and in a happy tone of voice, introduce them, "Bugsy, see the new chair? Yeah, sniff it!" and then let Bugsy investigate the chair.

New dogs and cats should be introduced in neutral territory, with both on a leash, and then supervise activities at home for several weeks until you're sure there won't be any problems.

Bulldogs snore and snort and snuffle.

Sleeping Habits

Bulldogs are usually delighted to share your bed or sleep on their own in your bedroom. But beware—most Bulldogs snore. They do not have a quiet, soft snore, either. It is a loud, regular snore. To the experienced Bulldog owner, this snore is music—an indication that all is right in the household. But if you are someone who must have absolute silence in your bedroom, your Bulldog must sleep at the other side of the house.

If, for some reason, it is impossible for your dog to share your bedroom, select a permanent spot for him to sleep. A laundry or utility room, if it is cool in the summer and warm in the winter, is ideal. A wire crate with a blanket or rug (not indoor-outdoor carpeting) for a bed is the next best thing to sharing your bed. This setup also gives the Bulldog a place of his own during the day. He can go there as he wishes, or you can put him there and close the door if things are happening in your home that a dog should not be part of.

Unpleasant Noises and Smells

Unfortunately, Bulldogs are prone to flatulence. This flatulence is not just a mild whiff of an odor, but can be a room-clearing, eye-watering, sneezing type of flatulence.

When my husband and I were still caring for Chesty, we were all (my husband and I, the two German Shepherd Dogs, and Chesty) in the living room one evening with all the dogs asleep on the floor. Suddenly Watachie, our older German Shepherd, got up and left the room. This was odd, because the German Shepherds liked to be close to us, but I figured maybe he had a bad dream.

A few seconds later, though, Michi, our younger German Shepherd, left the room—quickly! Just as I was ready to get up and check on both those dogs, a foul odor wafted over. I began to choke, my eyes watered, and my nose began to run! My husband soon smelled it too, and we left the room. Chesty, unaware that he had cleared the room, slept on.

Luckily, as we soon learned, when Bulldogs are fed a good-quality diet, the flatulence will decrease. It rarely disappears, but it will be less.

Bulldogs Need Exercise

Bulldogs are not high-energy dogs. Unlike the Border Collies, Australian Shepherds, or Labrador Retrievers, Bulldogs will be happy with a walk, a play session, and then a nap.

Although the Bulldog doesn't exactly crave exercise, he does need some. Exercise is necessary for maintaining his good health, just as it is for keeping his human friends in their prime. A walk at a brisk pace will be good for both you and your dog. Having your Bulldog chase and retrieve a ball gets him running about, as well. In addition, Bulldogs are prone to obesity, and exercise can help prevent that.

Bulldogs need exercise, but they can't tolerate heat. You'll have to be creative about how you exercise your dog.

Bulldogs Can't Stand the Heat

Bulldogs are bracycephalic (short-muzzled), and they tend to overheat easily. Dogs do not perspire over their entire body and are only cooled by panting and sweating through the pads of their feet, so extra precautions must be taken in hot weather. Walk your dog in the early morning or after sundown. *Never* leave your dog in the car, even if the windows are down. Stationary cars become very hot in just a few minutes and are virtual death traps.

Don't take your Bulldog for a walk in hot, humid weather or ask him to play ball then, either. Training classes should be in the morning or evening, and if you're going to a ball game, picnic, or family reunion in the heat, leave the Bulldog at home.

Bulldogs Like Other Pets

In addition to people, Bulldogs also like other dogs and cats if they grow up together or if they are introduced correctly. Bulldogs are not inherently aggressive (although they are creatures of habit), and if introduced in a positive manner, they will accept just about anything.

However, if another dog (or other animal) challenges a Bulldog, the Bulldog will not back down. This can cause problems, so make sure introductions are handled on leash and with praise, treats, games, and just enough obedience training to enforce good behavior. If you need help, call a dog trainer to give you a hand.

Bulldogs Love Life

Bulldogs have a definite joy about life. That smile is not just because the breed has a wide jaw; it's also representative of the Bulldog's attitude toward everything. Bulldogs feel there are fun and laughter everywhere. What a wonderful attitude!

Problem Bulldogs

Unfortunately, as with other breeds, there are some Bulldogs with problems. Every breed can produce the dog who may never be an enjoyable companion. But Bulldogs can be strong and powerful, so a problem dog could harm someone.

Beware of extremes—dogs who are too bold and aggressive or dogs who are very fearful and timid. Bulldogs who are too bold are not good examples of the

The Dog's Senses

The dog's eyes are designed so that he can see well in relative darkness, has excellent peripheral vision, and is very good at tracking moving objects—all skills that are important to a carnivore. Dogs also have good depth perception. Those advantages come at a price, though: Dogs are nearsighted and are slow to change the focus of their vision. It's a myth that dogs are colorblind. However, while they can see some (but not all) colors, their eyes were designed to most clearly perceive subtle shades of gray—an advantage when they are hunting in low light.

Dogs have about six times fewer taste buds on their tongue than humans do. They can taste sweet, sour, bitter, and salty flavors, but with so few taste buds, it's likely that their sense of taste is not very refined.

A dog's ears can swivel independently, like radar dishes, to pick up sounds and pinpoint their location. Dogs can locate a sound in $\frac{6}{100}$ of a second and hear sound four times farther away than we can (which is why there is no reason to yell at your dog). They can also hear sounds at far higher pitches than we can.

In their first few days of life, puppies primarily use their sense of touch to navigate their world. Whiskers on the face, above the eyes, and below the jaws are sensitive enough to detect changes in airflow. Dogs also have touch-sensitive nerve endings all over their bodies, including on their paws.

Smell may be a dog's most remarkable sense. Dogs have about 220 million scent receptors in their nose, compared to about 5 million in humans, and a large part of the canine brain is devoted to interpreting scent. Not only can dogs smell scents that are very faint, but they can also accurately distinguish between those scents. In other words, when you smell a pot of spaghetti sauce cooking, your dog probably smells tomatoes and onions and garlic and oregano and whatever else is in the pot.

Bulldogs can be silly and sweet. They love life and just want to be with you.

breed and may be dangerous to people. Bulldogs who are fearful and timid are poor representatives of the breed, too, and may bite when they are very afraid.

Good breeders are careful to choose dogs for breeding stock who are of good character and personality. Unfortunately, even careful breeders can sometimes still have a problem dog. Just don't feel sorry for that dog and take him on as a personal challenge. The risks are too great.

Although poor breeding practices create some of the bad dogs we see, people can also turn a good dog into a bad one. A dog who is neglected, unsocialized, teased, tormented, or treated unfairly for too long can turn into a dangerous dog.

If Bulldogs Could Choose Their Owners

If Bulldogs could choose their owners instead of the other way around, they would probably choose someone who enjoyed life as much as Bulldogs do. The ability to laugh at silly things would definitely be high on the Bulldog's list of owner requirements.

Bulldogs can be couch potatoes, and an owner who enjoys this too would make a Bulldog happy. But it's important for the Bulldog's health that he goes for walks, so the owner should be willing to walk the dog every day.

The Bulldog's owner must also have creative and innovative dog training skills, as well as lots of patience. Training is important, but not all Bulldogs agree. The owner also has to take the time to socialize his Bulldog and make sure his Bulldog is well behaved in public.

Most important, the very best owner for any Bulldog is an owner who loves his dog.

Chapter 4

Choosing Your Bulldog

The Bulldog you choose to join your family will be a vital part of your life for the next ten to twelve years. Bulldogs don't like to be ignored. This is not a dog who can be left in the backyard all the time or who will sleep quietly on a cushion as life goes on around her. Bulldogs like to be in the middle of everything, and will be!

It's very important that you choose the right Bulldog for you and your family. Although all Bulldogs have characteristics in common—short muzzles and a tendency to snore, for example—they also have individual personalities. Make an educated, well-researched choice and bring home the Bulldog who will best suit your needs.

Breeder, Rescue, Shelter, or Free?

Before you can bring a Bulldog home, you must find one. Bulldogs are not a prolific breed. Compared with other breeds, Bulldog litters are usually small, and most puppies must be delivered by cesarean section. The demand for puppies generally is greater than the supply. Have patience; your Bulldog is worth waiting for. Take time to find the puppy who is just what you have been dreaming about and enjoy the complete and nonjudgmental love and devotion that dog will offer.

Reputable Breeders

A reputable breeder is someone who breeds a specific breed of dogs and knows about their breed, has studied the genetics of dog breeding, and chooses the sire (father) and dam (mother) of each litter carefully.

Reputable breeders usually show their dogs in conformation dog shows so that the judges (who are also breeders) can evaluate their dogs. They will also have the necessary health checks done before breeding their dogs.

Most Bulldog breeders are sincere, honest people. They care about the welfare of their dogs and want only the best for you and the dog. A breeder who really cares about their dogs will screen potential buyers carefully because they are concerned about the future of their puppies. You may be asked to fill out an application and will be asked for references. If you don't sound like a good match for one of the puppies, the breeder will not sell you one. Don't take this personally. The breeder is not saying you're a bad person. They are simply saying that perhaps a Bulldog is not the right dog for you.

How do you find a reputable breeder? If you know someone who has a wonderful Bulldog, ask them where they got their dog. Ask the American Kennel Club for its list of breeders, or ask the Bulldog Club of America, which will direct you to breeders in your part of the country. (Contact information for both groups is in the appendix.)

If you buy a puppy (or dog) from a reputable breeder, they will be there for you in the future. They will be able to answer questions about their dogs and the breed in general, and will be able to guide you as your Bulldog grows through

Reputable breeders care about the well-being of every puppy they produce.

puppyhood and on into old age. The breeders of several of my dogs have turned into lifelong good friends.

Backyard Breeders

A backyard breeder is someone who has bred their dog but does not have the knowledge (or desire, or energy, or finances) to do what is necessary to produce the best dogs possible. Pet owners who pay a lot of money for their Bulldog sometimes decide to try to earn that money back by breeding the dog and selling the pups. These breeders do not research the pedigrees of their dogs to determine whether they are suitable breeding candidates, and the tests that can help predict the soundness of puppies are not done.

Sometimes a litter "appears" when the female has not been spayed and no efforts are made to keep her confined when she comes into season. The puppies may or may not be purebred, and the father (or fathers) of the litter may not be known.

Backyard breeders can produce some very nice puppies; it's happened before and will happen again. Unfortunately, they may also have less to offer you, especially when it comes to knowledge and experience. If you have problems with your puppy, will that person be able to help you?

Bulldog Rescue

Almost all breeds now have organizations dedicated to finding homes for dogs of their breed. Bulldogs lose their homes for various reasons. Perhaps a person bought a Bulldog puppy without first researching the breed and realized later that this was not a good match for their lifestyle. A Bulldog's owner may have passed away, or perhaps a couple divorced and neither wanted or could take the dog. Sometimes a Bulldog ends up in rescue because the owner didn't train their dog, socialize her, or teach her any household manners and now the dog has some problems.

Rescue groups evaluate the dogs coming into their program and then try to match them with new owners. They will ask you to fill out an application and supply a few references, just as breeders do. Although the rescue group may not be able to tell you much about the dog's genetic background, the evaluation process is usually pretty thorough, and they should be able to tell you whether the dog is housetrained, has any behavior problems, or is good with kids.

Adopting a dog from rescue is the choice for many people because not everyone wants a puppy. Lots of people also like the idea of saving a dog in need. By taking a dog who needs a home, they get a new family member and provide a needy dog with a secure, safe place to live.

Adult Bulldogs from rescue groups and shelters can make wonderful pets. Every Bulldog deserves a loving home.

Shelter Bulldogs

Dogs end up in shelters for many of the same reasons they end up in rescue programs. The primary difference between getting a dog from a rescue program and a shelter is that the people who work in a Bulldog rescue program know the breed and can evaluate the dog thoroughly. Shelters take in dogs of all breeds and mixes and of all ages, and are focused on getting those dogs adopted. They often cannot evaluate a dog as thoroughly as a rescue group can, and because the dogs live in runs rather than homes, their behavior is often unknown.

Shelters are also as good or as bad as the community that supports them. Some are wonderful, with caring employees and volunteers who keep the runs clean and give the animals as much attention as they can. Other shelters are horrible.

Ideally, a dog adopted from a shelter will be evaluated behaviorally, spayed or neutered, microchipped for identification, and up to date on all vaccinations.

"Free to Good Home" Bulldogs

Have you heard the saying, "If you get something for free, that's exactly what it's worth"? Why on earth would someone give away a Bulldog? Especially a Bulldog puppy? When females have small litters and need surgical help to give birth, puppies are too valuable to give away!

Any Bulldog offered for free should be viewed with skepticism. That cute puppy may be a Bulldog, but more likely she is a Bulldog mix. It's unlikely the puppy had any vaccinations or was given a health check before appearing in the cardboard box outside the grocery store. The half-grown puppy advertised in the classified ads for free was probably ignored in the backyard and so is not house-trained, is a rowdy teenager, and has no social skills.

A Bulldog offered for free is rarely a bargain. Dealing with already established behavior problems can be tough, plus the lack of history about the dog can make living with her difficult. The lack of any health information is also hard: Does she need vaccinations or not? Has she been spayed? Does she have any inherited health problems?

If you wish to save a Bulldog in need, especially one who might be facing death, that's fine. Just make sure you understand all the potential problems before you do so.

Finding Your Bulldog

Don't be in a hurry to find a Bulldog. It may take a little time. If you see a handsome, well-behaved Bulldog on a walk with her owners, ask them where they got her. They may be able to recommend a local breeder.

Check out local Bulldog clubs, too. You can find these on an Internet search. For example, type "Bulldog club + (your city and state)" into a search engine. Go to a club meeting or two and introduce yourself. When they learn you're serious about finding a good pet and companion, they will be more than willing to help you.

Once you have a few referrals to some breeders or rescue groups, call and ask for an appointment. Some may prefer to talk on the phone, while others may wish to meet you face to face. Ask the breeder a few questions: How long have you been breeding? Do you show your dogs? What health screenings do you do before breeding your dogs? What kind of sales contract do you use when selling your dogs?

Ask the rescue group some questions, too: Where did the dogs come from? How much do you know about the dogs? Do the dogs stay in foster homes or a kennel? Are the dogs spayed or neutered? Vaccinated? Microchipped?

The breeder or rescue volunteer will ask you some questions, too. Don't try to tell them what you think they want to hear; answer the questions honestly. Some questions might be: Have you owned a Bulldog before? Or any dog? If so, what happened to that dog? Where do you live? Do you own your own home? If not, will your landlord allow a Bulldog? Is there a homeowners' association that might forbid a Bulldog? Do you have a securely fenced yard? Will the Bulldog live in the house or out in the yard? The answers to these and other questions will determine whether the breeder or rescue volunteer will let you have a dog.

What Age?

Everyone loves puppies, right? Sure. But not everyone needs to live with a puppy or raise a puppy in order to have a great pet and companion. Sometimes the better choice may be an older puppy or an adult Bulldog.

Puppy or adult? Each has its advantages.

Bulldogs are good with children, but young, clumsy, untrained puppies and babies under 3 years are not a good combination. Neither is mature enough to comprehend the limitations of the other. If there are children under 3 years of age in your family, I suggest you look for a puppy at least 6 months old, or a young adult dog. It is not true that a pup must grow up with a child to accept the child. A little time and a little patience and even an older dog can be taught.

If you are busy, have some physical limitations, or are short of patience, you may want to consider an adult dog rather than a puppy. Puppies are cute and snuggly, but they require a great deal of supervision, socialization, training, and patience.

What Color?

You had your heart set on a white puppy, but there are no white puppies. Should you look further for the white puppy? If the only thing that's preventing you from selecting one puppy from a litter is color, I suggest you pick the one who pleases you most in this particular litter.

Color really is not important, and soon you will have forgotten you ever wanted a white one as the brindle one (or the brown one or the red and white one) finds her way into your heart.

Male or Female?

Should you get a male or a female? Both sexes make equally good pets, and neutering the male or spaying the female prevents many problems as your Bulldog grows older. So often it is a purely personal decision as to what sex to get. Many men prefer female dogs because they feel a stronger bond with a female, and many women prefer a male dog.

If possible, get to know a few Bulldogs before you make any decision and see if either sex appeals to you more. You may be surprised.

Choosing Your Bulldog Puppy

Service dog trainers have developed puppy tests that help them evaluate puppies' responses to specific stimuli and choose puppies for certain service dog work. The service dog trainers are then able to train only those dogs who have the temperament, character, and personality traits that are best suited for service dog work.

Although Bulldogs are rarely used as service dogs, puppy tests can help you, too, because these tests can help you choose the best dog for you, your family, and your goals for the dog. The tests are best done when the puppy is 6 to 7 weeks old. Many breeders do puppy tests, so if your breeder does, just ask if you can watch. If they normally don't test the puppies, ask if you can do it. They may just be interested enough in the results to let you try.

They're all cute! Puppy tests will help you choose among the pups.

Puppy Temperament Test

Have your paper at hand and make notes as you go along, or better yet, have someone else make notes for you. Test each puppy individually. Don't look at your notes until you're done.

Walk away. Place the puppy on the ground at your feet. Stand up and walk away. Does the puppy:

a. Follow you.
b. Put herself underfoot, climbing on your feet.
c. Do a belly crawl to follow you.
d. Ignore you and go the other direction.

Call the puppy. Move away from the puppy, then bend over and call her, spreading your hands and arms wide to encourage her. Does the puppy:

a. Come to you, tail wagging.
b. Chase you so fast that you don't have a chance to call her.
c. Come slowly or crawl on her belly to you.
d. Ignore you.

Look at the Whole Litter

On a sheet of paper, list all the puppies. If several look alike, put different color ribbons on them. Now, without getting involved (no petting or playing), just watch the entire litter. There may be three or four puppies in a Bulldog litter. By 6 weeks of age, the puppies will be playing with each other, bouncing around, tripping over each other and their own clumsy paws.

As you watch, make some notes about their behavior. The boldest puppy, who is often also the biggest, is usually the first to do anything. She is the first to the food, the first to check out a new toy, and the first to investigate anything new. She would not be a good choice for someone who lives alone and works long hours, nor would she be a good dog for someone with a less-than-dominant personality.

Bulldogs rarely have fearful personalities, but it can happen. The fearful puppy will sit in the corner by herself, just watching what her brothers and sisters are doing. She may duck her head. Although some fearful puppies can

Gentle restraint. Pick up the puppy and gently roll her over so she's on her back in your arms. Place a hand on her chest to gently restrain her for thirty seconds—no longer. Does she:

a. Struggle for a few seconds, then relax.
b. Struggle for the entire thirty seconds.
c. Cry, tuck her tail up, and perhaps urinate.
d. Struggle for fifteen seconds, stop, then look at you or look away.

Lifting. When the puppy is on the ground, place both hands under her rib cage and lift her paws off the ground for thirty seconds. Does the puppy:

a. Quietly accept it with just a little wiggling.
b. Struggle for at least fifteen seconds.
c. Accept it with a tucked tail.
d. Struggle for more than fifteen seconds.

Toss a ball. With the puppy close to you, show her a ball and then toss it just a few feet away. Does the puppy:

a. Dash after it, pick it up, and bring it back to you.
b. Bring it back but doesn't want to give it back to you.
c. Go after it but does not pick it up, or gets distracted.
d. Pick it up but walk away.

come out of their shell with a calm, caring, knowledgeable owner, these dogs usually retain some of their fear their whole lives. These dogs are not good for noisy, active households or for first-time dog owners.

Most puppies fall somewhere in between these two extremes. In one situation the puppy may be bold and outgoing, and in another she may fall back to watch. While you're watching, look to see who is the crybaby, who is the troublemaker, and who always gets the toy. Jot down notes.

Now it's time for the test. You'll find it in the box above.

Looking at the Results

There are no right or wrong answers. This is a guide to help you choose the right puppy for you—and even then, this is only a guide. Puppies can change as they grow up.

Watching how the puppies interact will tell you a lot about their personalities.

The puppy who scored mostly A's is a middle-of-the-pack dog in terms of dominance. This is not the most dominant puppy or the most submissive. If she also scored an A in the ball test, this puppy will suit most families with children or active couples. This puppy should accept training well, and although she may have some challenges during adolescence, she will grow up to be a nice dog.

The puppy who scored mostly A's and B's will be a little more dominant, a little more pushy. If she scored a B or a D on the ball test, you may find training to be somewhat of a challenge.

The puppy who scored mostly B's is a more dominant puppy. She could be a great working dog with the right owner. She needs an owner who has a more forceful personality; she is not the right dog for a passive person. She will need structured training from puppyhood on into adulthood.

The puppy who scored mostly C's will need special handling as this puppy is very worried about life. She could, if pushed too far, bite out of fear. She needs a calm environment and a calm, confidant owner.

The puppy who scored C's and D's may have trouble bonding with people. However, if she finds the right owner, she will bond and will be very devoted. This puppy needs calm, careful, patient training.

The puppy who scored mostly D's doesn't think she needs people. She is very self-confident and will need to spend a lot of time with her owner so that she can develop a relationship. If she spends too much time alone, she may not bond with a person at all.

Now What?

After looking at the puppies, figuring out the results, and perhaps narrowing the litter down to one or two puppies, now what? Which puppy appeals to you the most? Which puppy keeps returning to you? Which one makes your heart go thump-thump? Which puppy makes you laugh out loud?

Although these tests can help narrow your choices, you still need to listen to your heart. So think logically and then let your heart work with your brain to choose the right puppy for you.

Choosing an Adult Bulldog

A puppy is a blank slate. She is the result of her genetics and the care she's received as a baby, but other than that, she's just ready for the world. An adult Bulldog, on the other hand, is already formed. What you see is what you're going to get.

The adult Bulldog also has a history. Perhaps she was in a loving home and lost that home due to a divorce or a death in the family. She may have been in a home where she was neglected or even mistreated. The things that happened to her have shaped who she is. She may always be worried about large men with sticks in their hands, or she may always be attracted to older women.

If you decide to adopt an adult Bulldog, it's important to find out as much as you can about the dog and her first home so that you can help her make the adjustment to your home. For example, if the shelter people say she appears to be afraid of brooms, once she's in your home, ask a trainer or behaviorist for help desensitizing her to brooms.

Tests used on baby puppies do not work on adult dogs; so when adopting an adult dog, you need to rely on any information you can get from the people who have been caring for her. Then, before you make a decision, spend some time with the dog. Take her for a walk. Sit on the grass and give her a belly rub. Toss a toy for her to play with. Get to know her before you make any big decision. After all, this dog will be a part of your family for years to come.

When you're choosing an adult dog, just spend some time with her and see how you get along.

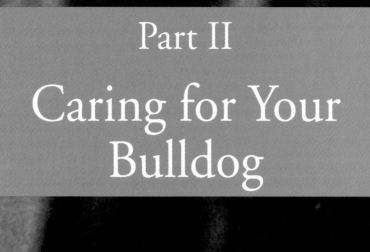

Part II
Caring for Your Bulldog

Chapter 5

Bringing Your Bulldog Home

A new Bulldog—how exciting! If you've had a Bulldog before, you know how much your life is going to change. But if this is your first Bulldog, you have no idea yet. Bulldogs are unique among dogs. They're silly and yet dignified, affectionate and loyal. They snort and snore and pass gas, but at the same time they will love you with all their being.

Before you bring home your new best friend, you need to make sure you're ready for him. Your house, yard, and garage need to be puppy-proofed for safety, and the fence should be checked for any gaps or loose boards. You may also need to go shopping.

Safety Is Important

When your new Bulldog comes home, he's not going to know where he is, who everyone in your family is, and why he's there. He may settle in with no problems at all, or he may be a little stressed. If your Bulldog is a baby puppy, he may be curious and may want to explore the house, yard, and garage. If your new Bulldog is an adult, he may be worried and may try to escape from the yard. In any case, it's very important that you make sure everything—house, yard, and garage—are safe and secure before you bring home your new Bulldog.

A Secure Yard

Your Bulldog will be happiest spending time in the house with you. However, he will also enjoy some time outside basking in the sun or snoozing in the shade. Your yard needs to be safe and the fence secure.

The yard should be free of anything your Bulldog might decide to turn into a toy, including gardening tools, kids' toys, and pool tools, toys, and supplies. Bulldogs have powerful jaws, and if your dog decides to chew on anything, it will be destroyed. Besides causing damage, your dog may also hurt himself.

Bulldogs can't jump a fence, but they can climb up (for instance, on a nearby wood pile) and get over that way.

Make sure there are no chemicals around that might tempt your dog. Put away all insecticides, fertilizers, herbicides, and anything else you use in the yard or pool. When stored away, put them behind a good latch or better yet, a lock.

The fence also needs to be strong and secure. Although Bulldogs are not known for their jumping abilities, they can climb. If the firewood is piled up against the fence, your Bulldog may decide to climb up and over. In addition, Bulldogs are strong. When faced with a weak fence and something interesting outside the fence, your Bulldog may decide to go right on through it.

Once you have made your yard as safe and secure as it can be, walk around and take another look at it from your Bulldog's point of view. Bend down or get down on your knees. Do you see that cord dangling from the spa motor? A Bulldog puppy will chew that. See the potted plants on the porch with leaves dangling from the pots? Those will be great fun to chew up. How about the ties that hold the cushions on the lawn chairs? Those are fun to pull on. Double-check to make sure your Bulldog will be safe and can cause as few problems as possible.

When to Bring Your Puppy Home

Pick a time when you will be at home for several days. Your puppy needs to get to know you, to become acclimated to his new home, and to get comfortable with his daily schedule of walks, playtime, and perhaps his new food (don't change food, unless it's absolutely necessary, for several days, and then change it gradually).

Puppy Essentials

You'll need to go shopping *before* you bring your puppy home. There are many, many adorable and tempting items at pet supply stores, but these are the basics.

- **Food and water dishes.** Look for bowls that are wide and low or weighted in the bottom so that they will be harder to tip over. Stainless steel bowls are a good choice because they are easy to clean (plastic never gets completely clean) and almost impossible to break. Avoid bowls that place the food and water side by side in one unit—it's too easy for your dog to get his water dirty that way.
- **Leash.** A six-foot leather leash will be easy on your hands and very strong.
- **Collar.** Start with a nylon buckle collar. For a perfect fit, you should be able to insert two fingers between the collar and your pup's neck. Your dog will need larger collars as he grows up.
- **Crate.** Choose a sturdy crate that is easy to clean and large enough for your puppy to stand up, turn around, and lie down in.
- **Nail cutters.** Get a good, sharp pair that are the appropriate size for the nails you will be cutting. Your dog's breeder or veterinarian can give you some guidance here.
- **Grooming tools.** Different kinds of dogs need different kinds of grooming tools. See chapter 7 for advice on what to buy.
- **Chew toys.** Dogs *must* chew, especially puppies. Make sure you get things that won't break or crumble off in little bits, which the dog can choke on. Very hard plastic bones are a good choice. Dogs love rawhide bones, too, but pieces of the rawhide can get caught in your dog's throat, so they should only be allowed when you are there to supervise.
- **Toys.** Watch for sharp edges and unsafe items such as plastic eyes that can be swallowed. Many toys come with squeakers, which dogs can also tear out and swallow. All dogs will eventually destroy their toys; as each toy is torn apart, replace it with a new one.

He needs some free time to explore. He needs to be held and loved. Just imagine yourself in his place: He has no idea where he is and who you are. Your puppy can't talk, and he can't really understand what you are saying. Everything is new

Your swimming pool is not safe for a Bulldog, but your dog will probably appreciate a shallow pool of his own.

and different. It takes time, but the time you spend with him now will help him learn to trust you and be a happy, confident animal living a wonderful life.

Choosing Pet Professionals

Finally, before you bring your puppy home, select a few pet professionals to help you care for your Bulldog. You will need a veterinarian, a dog trainer, and a pet sitter or boarding kennel.

You can find these professionals by asking dog-owning friends about whom they have done business with and whom they recommend. Is there someone they suggest you should avoid? Once you have a few names, call and make an appointment. In most cases, it's wiser to have an established relationship with a professional *before* you need their help.

Veterinarian

Your Bulldog will need a veterinarian to care for his health. Select the veterinarian as you would your own private physician or pediatrician. Ask if they are comfortable treating Bulldogs; not all veterinarians are. The vet should be aware of the health problems faced by Bulldogs and how to treat them.

Ask the veterinarian what their payment policies are and what credit cards they accept. Are they available after hours and on weekends? If not, do they recommend a local emergency clinic? What else is important to you? This is the time to ask.

Puppy-Proofing Your Home

You can prevent much of the destruction puppies can cause and keep your new dog safe by looking at your home and yard from a dog's point of view. Get down on all fours and look around. Do you see loose electrical wires, cords dangling from the blinds, or chewable shoes on the floor? Your pup will see them too!

In the kitchen:

- Put all knives and other utensils away in drawers.
- Get a trash can with a tight-fitting lid.
- Put all household cleaners in cupboards that close securely; consider using childproof latches on the cabinet doors.

In the bathroom:

- Keep all household cleaners, medicines, vitamins, shampoos, bath products, perfumes, makeup, nail polish remover, and other personal products in cupboards that close securely; consider using childproof latches on the cabinet doors.
- Get a trash can with a tight-fitting lid.
- Don't use toilet bowl cleaners that release chemicals into the bowl every time you flush.
- Keep the toilet bowl lid down.
- Throw away potpourri and any solid air fresheners.

In the bedroom:

- Securely put away all potentially dangerous items, including medicines and medicine containers, vitamins and supplements, perfumes, and makeup.
- Put all your jewelry, barrettes, and hairpins in secure boxes.
- Pick up all socks, shoes, and other chewables.

Dog Trainer

A dog trainer will teach you how to train your Bulldog and will help you as you progress with your training. The trainer can also assist you as you socialize your

In the rest of the house:

- Tape up or cover electrical cords; consider childproof covers for unused outlets.
- Knot or tie up any dangling cords from curtains, blinds, and the telephone.
- Securely put away all potentially dangerous items, including medicines and medicine containers, vitamins and supplements, cigarettes, cigars, pipes and pipe tobacco, pens, pencils, felt-tip markers, craft and sewing supplies, and laundry products.
- Put all houseplants out of reach.
- Move breakable items off low tables and shelves.
- Pick up all chewable items, including television and electronics remote controls, cell phones, MP3 players, shoes, socks, slippers and sandals, food, dishes, cups and utensils, toys, books and magazines, and anything else that can be chewed on.

In the garage:

- Store all gardening supplies and pool chemicals out of reach of the dog.
- Store all antifreeze, oil, and other car fluids securely, and clean up any spills by hosing them down for at least ten minutes.
- Put all dangerous substances on high shelves or in cupboards that close securely; consider using childproof latches on the cabinet doors.
- Pick up and put away all tools.
- Sweep the floor for nails and other small, sharp items.

In the yard:

- Put the gardening tools away after each use.
- Make sure the kids put away their toys when they're finished playing.
- Keep the pool covered or otherwise restrict your pup's access to it when you're not there to supervise.
- Secure the cords on backyard lights and other appliances.
- Inspect your fence thoroughly. If there are any gaps or holes in the fence, fix them.
- Make sure you have no toxic plants in the garden.

Bulldog and introduce him to the world around him. The trainer will also be available to help you if you encounter any problems along the way.

The trainer you choose needs to like Bulldogs and be aware of their training challenges. You can ask other Bulldog owners whom they recommend, or ask if your veterinarian knows a good trainer. Once you find a trainer, ask if you can watch a couple of classes. Make sure you will be comfortable in the class and with that person's training techniques.

Pet Sitter or Boarding Kennel

You will need someone to watch your Bulldog when you won't be home. You may need to make a business trip or go on a vacation when your Bulldog can't go

> **TIP**
>
> **Find a Pet Sitter**
>
> To find an experienced, professional pet sitter in your area, check out the Web sites of Pet Sitters International (www.petsit.com) and the National Association of Professional Pet Sitters (www.petsitters.org).

with you. Although many people ask a friend or neighbor to watch their dog, far too many catastrophes have happened in these situations.

A professional pet sitter will come out to your house a couple of times each day to feed, water, and play with your Bulldog. They can even take him for walks, too. The pet sitter will also pick up the newspapers and the mail. The positive aspect of this service is that your dog remains in the comfortable surroundings of his home. The negative is that for most of the day and night your dog is alone. What will happen if there is an emergency?

Puppies can get into a lot of trouble. The easiest way to avoid it is not to give them free run of the house.

If you decide to use a boarding kennel, your dog will stay at the kennel. He will not be at home, but he will be closely supervised.

Obviously there are pros and cons to both situations. You will need to find out which will work better for you and your dog.

Crate Training

With a small puppy, it is best to confine him to specific areas until he is completely housetrained. The ideal plan is to have a place where

Toys are not optional. Dogs need toys all their lives.

he can be confined in the kitchen or family room—someplace where he is still part of the family. He can have freedom to roam around for a short time and under constant supervision, right after he has eliminated outside. As he grows and matures, he will be allowed more freedom.

The easiest and most effective way to confine a Bulldog puppy is to get a metal wire crate (he will chew on plastic or soft sided crates) that's at least twenty-four inches wide, thirty-six inches long, and twenty-six inches high. Place it where the puppy is to sleep; make sure this area is warm and free of drafts. Confine the puppy except for those times when he's supervised. Leave the crate door open when the puppy is out so that he can return at will. But bear in mind that a puppy, or an adult dog, cannot be crated all day.

Is a Crate a Canine Jail?

Crates serve many functions. Many people use a crate to housetrain their puppy or adult dog. This is an excellent idea because it enables you to train your pet faster and with less trauma, mental and physical. The crate can also be a safe haven for pets who are destructive while the owner is away. It makes travel with your pet much safer for you and the animal, as well.

Most dogs do not resent a crate, but rather find it to be a safe and secure retreat. Many people who use a crate for housetraining will see their dog lying in the crate with the door open when he is tired and wants someplace quiet to sleep. Other times, when the hustle and bustle of the home is reaching a high point, the dog may voluntarily retire to his crate with a toy to chew on. I believe crates are one of the very best training tools. Don't feel guilty about using one.

Chapter 6

Feeding Your Bulldog

Most Bulldogs believe everything that is chewable can be eaten. Many Bulldogs even like fresh fruits, especially oranges and watermelon. I do not recommend that she be given these fruits freely or frequently, but every once in a while, smile, give her a small piece of watermelon and watch her chomp and enjoy. So, the problem of feeding a Bulldog isn't finding something she will eat, but searching through the myriad brands, formulas, and consistencies to find what is best for her and readily available.

Dog food is a lucrative business. Big sums of money are spent on advertising and developing foods that are palatable and healthy. On the practical side of the coin, the cost of these foods must be reasonable and within the reach of the average consumer.

Nutritional Building Blocks

Nutrition is a constantly ongoing process that starts at conception (with the mother dog's diet) and ends only with death. Everything that is consumed becomes part of the dog's daily nutrition, whether it's good for her or not. In other words, anything your Bulldog eats and digests (including snails, worms, or the kids' peanut butter sandwich) can give her some kind of nutrition. However, what the dog eats, the food's actual digestibility, and how the dog's body uses that food can all affect the actual nutrition gained by eating.

Although your Bulldog can eat many things, including a lot of materials that may not be good for her, there are some substances she must eat regularly to keep her healthy. These can be a part of the commercial dog food you feed her, part of a homemade diet, or in the supplements added to her food.

Protein

Proteins are a varied group of biological compounds that affect many different functions in your Bulldog's body, including the immune system, cell structure, and growth. As omnivores (dogs eat meat as well as some plant materials), dogs can digest protein from several sources. The most common are meats, grains, dairy products, and legumes. Recommendations vary as to how much of the dog's diet should be protein, but in general, most nutritionists agree that a diet that contains between 20 and 40 percent quality protein is good for a dog.

Carbohydrates

Carbohydrates, like proteins, have many functions in the dog's body, including serving as structural components of cells. However, the most important function is as an energy source. Carbohydrates can be obtained from many sources, including tubers (such as potatoes and sweet potatoes), plants (such as greens like broccoli and collard greens), and cereals. However, dogs do not have the necessary digestive enzymes to adequately digest all cereal grains. Therefore, the

Good nutrition is the foundation for solid structure as your dog grows.

TIP
Don't forget to wash your dog's bowl after each meal. The leftover food particles and her saliva can cause a bacteria buildup in the bowl. Although she may not get sick right away, if the bacteria continue to build, she will. The water bowl should be cleaned regularly, too.

better sources of carbohydrates are tubers and noncitrus fruits, such as apples and bananas. Most experts recommend that a dog's diet contain from 20 to 40 percent carbohydrates of the right kind.

Fat

Fats have many uses in the body. They are the most important way the body stores energy. Fats also make up some of the structural elements of cells and are vital to the absorption of several vitamins. Certain fats are also beneficial in keeping the skin and coat healthy. Fats in dog foods are found primarily in meat and dairy products. Recommended levels are from 10 to 20 percent.

Vitamins

Vitamins are vital elements necessary for growth and the maintenance of life. There are two classes of vitamins: water-soluble and fat-soluble. Water-soluble vitamins include the B-complex vitamins and vitamin C. Fat-soluble vitamins include A, D, E, and K.

Water-Soluble Vitamins

These vitamins are absorbed by the body during digestion using the water found in the dog's food. Although it's usually a good idea to allow the dog to drink water whenever she's thirsty, additional water is not needed for digestion of these vitamins, because the water in the dog's body is sufficient as long as the dog is not dehydrated. Excess water-soluble vitamins are excreted from the body in the urine, so it's difficult to oversupplement these vitamins—although too much vitamin C can cause diarrhea.

The B vitamins serve a number of functions, including the metabolism of carbohydrates and amino acids. The B vitamins are involved in many biochemical processes, and deficiencies can show up as weight loss, slow growth, dry and flaky skin, or anemia, depending on the specific deficiency. The B vitamins can be obtained from meat and dairy products, beans, and eggs.

Vitamin C is a powerful antioxidant and, at the same time, a controversial vitamin. Some respected sources state that it is not a required dietary supplement for dogs, yet others regard C as a miracle vitamin. Some feel it can help prevent hip dysplasia and other potential problems, but these claims have not been proven. Dogs can produce a certain amount of vitamin C in their bodies, but this amount is often not sufficient, especially if the dog is under stress from work, injury, or illness.

Fat-Soluble Vitamins

These vitamins require some fats in the dog's diet for adequate absorption. Fats are in the meat in your dog's diet and are added to commercial dog foods. Excess fat-soluble vitamins are stored in the body's fat. Excess vitamins of this type can cause problems, including toxicity. These vitamins should be added to the diet with care.

Vitamin A deficiencies show up as slow or retarded growth, reproductive failure, and skin and vision problems. Green and yellow vegetables are excellent sources of vitamin A, as are carrots, fish oils, and animal livers. The vegetables should be lightly cooked so that the dog can digest them.

Vitamin D is needed for the correct absorption of calcium and phosphorus, and is necessary for the growth and development of bones and teeth and for muscle strength. Many dogs will produce a certain amount of vitamin D when exposed to sunlight; however, often that is not enough, and supplementation is needed. Balanced dog foods will generally have vitamin D in sufficient quantities.

Vitamin E is a powerful antioxidant that also works with several enzymes in the body. It has been shown to be effective in maintaining heart health and the immune system. It is also vital to other bodily systems, including the blood, nerves, muscles, and skin.

Vitamin K is needed for the proper clotting of blood. It is also important for healthy bones. Vitamin K is produced in the intestinal tract, and normally supplementation is not needed. However, if the dog is having digestion problems or is on antibiotics, supplementation may be required. Vitamin K can be found in dark green vegetables, including kale and spinach. These should be lightly cooked before feeding them to your dog.

How much to feed your dog depends on her age and activity level.

Your dog needs access to fresh, clean water all day, every day.

Minerals

Minerals, like vitamins, are necessary for life and physical well-being. Minerals can affect the body in many ways. A deficiency of calcium can lead to rickets, a deficiency of manganese can cause reproductive failure, and a zinc deficiency can lead to growth retardation and skin problems.

Many minerals are tied in with vitamins; in other words, a vitamin deficiency will also result in a mineral deficiency. For example, an adequate amount of vitamin B_{12} ensures there is also an adequate amount of cobalt because cobalt, a mineral, is a constituent of B_{12}.

Minerals are normally added to commercial dog foods. If you're feeding a homemade diet, it can be supplemented with a vitamin and mineral tablet to make sure the dog has sufficient minerals.

Water

It may seem like common sense to say that your Bulldog will need water, but the importance of water cannot be emphasized enough. Water makes up about 70 percent of a dog's weight. Water facilitates the generation of energy, the transportation of nutrients, and the disposal of wastes. Water is in the bloodstream, in the eyes, in the cerebrospinal fluid, and in the gastrointestinal tract. Water is vital to all of the body's functions in some way. Don't forget to clean your dog's water bowl every day.

Commercial Dog Foods

Dog food sales in the United States are a huge business with tremendous competition among manufacturers. Dog owners should understand that as a big business, the goals of these companies include making a profit. Although advertising may show a dog and owner in a warm and fuzzy, heart-tugging moment,

Reading Dog Food Labels

Dog food labels are not always easy to read, but if you know what to look for, they can tell you a lot about what your dog is eating.

- The label should have a statement saying the dog food meets or exceeds the American Association of Feed Control Officials (AAFCO) nutritional guidelines. If the dog food doesn't meet AAFCO guidelines, it can't be considered complete and balanced, and can cause nutritional deficiencies.
- The guaranteed analysis lists the minimum percentages of crude protein and crude fat and the maximum percentages of crude fiber and water. AAFCO requires a minimum of 18 percent crude protein for adult dogs and 22 percent crude protein for puppies on a dry matter basis (that means with the water removed; canned foods will have less protein because they have more water). Dog food must also have a minimum of 5 percent crude fat for adults and 8 percent crude fat for puppies.
- The ingredients list the most common item in the food first, and so on until you get to the least common item, which is listed last.
- Look for a dog food that lists an animal protein source first, such as chicken or poultry meal, beef or beef by-products, and that has other protein sources listed among the top five ingredients. That's because a food that lists chicken, wheat, wheat gluten, corn, and wheat fiber as the first five ingredients has more chicken than wheat, but may not have more chicken than all the grain products put together.
- Other ingredients may include a carbohydrate source, fat, vitamins and minerals, preservatives, fiber, and sometimes other additives purported to be healthy.
- Some brands may add artificial colors, sugar, and fillers—all of which should be avoided.

the nutrition your dog might get from the food being advertised has nothing to do with that heart-tugging moment. It's all about getting you to buy the food.

Dog owners must be wise consumers, and we cannot let the pet food recall of 2007 fade into memory. Read the dog food labels, check out the manufacturers' Web sites, check the recall lists, and talk to dog food experts, including your veterinarian if they have a background in nutrition.

Bulldogs do well on a food with plenty of protein. That meat builds muscle.

A good-quality food is necessary for your Bulldog's health. Dog foods vary in quality, from the very good to the terrible. To make sure you are using a high-quality food, read the labels on the packages (see the box on page 65). Make sure the food offers the levels of protein, carbohydrates, and fats recommended earlier in this chapter.

Read the list of ingredients, too. If one of the first ingredients listed is by-products, be leery of the food. By-products are the parts of slaughtered animals that are not muscle meat—lungs, spleen, kidneys, brain, liver, blood, bone, fatty tissue, stomach, and intestines. Dog food manufacturers can meet protein requirements by including by-products, but they are inferior forms of protein that do not metabolize as completely in the dog's body.

Bulldogs do well on a dog food that uses a muscle meat as the first ingredient. Muscle meats are listed on the label simply as beef, chicken, fish, and so on. Steer away from foods with a lot of soy or soy products, as these are thought to contribute to stomach gas, which can lead to bloat (for more on this disease, see chapter 8).

Homemade Diets

Dog owners who feed homemade diets usually do so because they are concerned about the quality of commercially available foods. Some owners do not want their dogs eating the additives or preservatives that are in many commercial dog

Pet Food vs. People Food

Many of the foods we eat are excellent sources of nutrients—after all, we do just fine on them. But dogs, like us, need the right combination of meat and other ingredients for a complete and balanced diet, and a bowl of meat doesn't provide that. In the wild, dogs eat the fur, skin, bones, and guts of their prey, and even the contents of the stomach.

This doesn't mean your dog can't eat what you eat. A little meat, dairy, bread, some fruits, or vegetables as a treat are great. Just remember, we're talking about the same food you eat, not the gristly, greasy leftovers you would normally toss in the trash. Stay away from sugar, too, and remember that chocolate and alcohol are toxic to dogs.

If you want to share your food with your dog, be sure the total amount you give her each day doesn't make up more than 15 percent of her diet, and that the rest of what you feed her is a top-quality complete and balanced dog food. (More people food could upset the balance of nutrients in the commercial food.)

Can your dog eat an entirely homemade diet? Certainly, if you are willing to work at it. Any homemade diet will have to be carefully balanced, with all the right nutrients in just the right amounts. It requires a lot of research to make a proper homemade diet, but it can be done. It's best to work with a veterinary nutritionist.

foods. Others cook their dog's food so that they can control exactly what their dogs eat. Many people began making homemade diets for their dogs during and after the pet food recalls of 2007.

There are many resources now available to dog owners who wish to feed a homemade diet. Just make sure the diet is complete and contains all the nutrients your dog needs. Keep a line of communication open with your veterinarian so that they can monitor your dog's continued good health.

Feeding Your Dog

Some dog owners like to fill a bowl with dog food and leave it out all day, letting the dog munch at will. Although it may be convenient, it is not a good idea for several reasons. First of all, outdoors the bowl of food may attract birds, squirrels, and ants. Indoors, the food may attract ants, flies, and cockroaches. In addition, the food could become rancid.

When you are housetraining your puppy, free feeding makes it difficult to set up a routine. Your puppy will need to relieve herself after eating, and if she munches all day long, you won't be able to tell when she should go outside.

Last, but certainly not least, psychologically your dog needs to know that you are the giver of the food. How better for her to learn it than when you hand her a bowl twice a day? If the food is always available, you are not the one giving it. It's always there—at least as far as your dog is concerned.

How Much?

Each and every Bulldog needs a different amount of food. When puppies are growing quickly, they will need more food. When your Bulldog is all grown up, if she continues eating that same amount of food, she will get fat. The dog's individual body metabolism, activity rate, and lifestyle all affect her nutritional needs.

Feeding a puppy at specific times each day will greatly help with the housetraining. What goes in on schedule comes out on schedule.

Bulldogs have a tendency to become overweight. Don't let that cute face push you into the habit of overindulging your dog.

Most dog food manufacturers print a chart on the bag showing how much to feed your dog. It's important to note that these are *suggested* guidelines. If your puppy or dog is soft, round, and fat, cut back on the food. If your dog is thin and always hungry, give her more food. A healthy, well-nourished dog will have bright eyes, an alert expression, a shiny coat, supple skin, and energy to work and play.

Meal Times

Most experts recommend that puppies eat two to three times a day. Most adult dogs do very well with two meals, ten or twelve hours apart, so feed your dog after you eat breakfast and then again after you have dinner.

While you are eating, don't feed your Bulldog from the table or toss her scraps; it will cause her to beg from anyone at the table—a very bad habit. Don't toss her leftovers as you are cooking, either. That can lead to begging and even stealing in the kitchen. Bulldogs are bright enough to figure out how to open cupboard doors and are bold enough to raid the kitchen trash can.

Treats

An occasional dog biscuit or some training treats will not spoil your Bulldog's appetite, but don't get in the habit of offering treats just for the pleasure of it.

Many dogs are overweight, and obesity is a leading killer of dogs. Unfortunately, with their ever-present appetite and their love of comfort, Bulldogs do tend to gain weight easily.

When you do offer treats, offer either treats made specifically for dogs or something that is low in calories and nutritious, like a carrot. Don't offer candy, cookies, leftover tacos, or anything like that. Your Bulldog doesn't need sugar, chocolate is deadly for dogs, and spicy foods can cause diarrhea and an upset stomach. Play it safe and give your Bulldog good-quality, nutritious snacks very sparingly.

If you are using treats to train your dog, use good ones—nutritious treats—and cut back on all other treats. Training treats can be tiny pieces of cooked meats such as chicken or beef; just dice the pieces very small. Cheese is also a great training treat. Cut it into tiny pieces, put it in a sandwich bag, and toss it in the freezer. Bring out a few frozen pieces for each training session. (Cheese is easy to handle when frozen, and your dog won't mind.)

Five Mistakes to Avoid

1. Don't feed your dog chocolate, raisins, grapes, macadamia nuts, onions, or any highly spiced, greasy, or salty foods. The first five can be toxic, and spicy or junk foods can lead to an upset stomach.
2. Don't believe all the dog food advertising you see and hear. Keep in mind that advertising has one goal: to get you to buy that product.
3. If you change foods for any reason, don't do it all at once. Mix the foods so that the dog has 25 percent new food and 75 percent old food for a week. Then feed half and half for a week. Finally, offer 75 percent new food and 25 percent old food for a week. This will decrease the chances of an upset stomach. If your Bulldog develops diarrhea during the switching process, you're making the change too quickly.
4. Don't feed your dog from the table. This will lead to begging and even stealing. Feed her in her own spot after the family has eaten.
5. Raw food diets are very popular, including those that recommend giving the dog raw bones. Be careful giving your Bulldog any bones except raw beef knucklebones. Adult Bulldogs have powerful jaws and could crack, splinter, and ingest smaller bones with the potential of damage to the gastrointestinal system.

Chapter 7

Grooming Your Bulldog

Bulldogs really enjoy being groomed (although some do protest nail trimming), and many especially enjoy taking baths. In fact, if you bathe your Bulldog in the bathtub, be sure to close your bathroom door tightly when taking your own bath or he may try to share the tub with you.

The Bulldog has a smooth, short coat and is naturally a reasonably clean dog. Because of this short coat, many people think grooming is not necessary. But even short coats need care.

Grooming your Bulldog should be regular and routine, just as it is for you. Don't wait until your puppy has grown to get started. Instead, begin when he is young and he will grow up cooperative.

The Daily Ritual

Stand the puppy on a bench or table, or any flat surface that is the best height for your comfort. Assure the puppy that he isn't being punished and this is a special time just for him. Note the sheen in his coat. Check for any bare spots in his coat or skin lesions. Are his eyes clear and free of discharge? Is his nose soft and free of crust? Are the insides of his ears smooth or is the skin rough, flaky, and inflamed? Note his feet—are they swollen, especially between his toes?

This seems like a lot of checking, but before you realize, it will become a regular habit to observe all these points, and you will immediately be aware of any abnormalities that can indicate potential problems.

Bulldogs enjoy grooming because they are people dogs and enjoy anything that involves attention from those they love. Grooming is an exercise in observation and prevention, providing a healthy, happy, clean dog. I have recommended daily grooming, but if your skills of observation are keen and your dog does not have any problems, it is no sin to reduce the frequency to two or three times a week.

Brushing

The next step in the daily grooming ritual will be brushing. How much and how long will depend on the condition of the coat. Your dog's coat is a good barometer of his health. Is the shedding minimal or is it excessive? If the shedding is not seasonal excess, then there must be another reason—stress, worms, fleas, diet? All these and more can cause excess shedding, and only your veterinarian can make an accurate diagnosis.

Only seasonal shedding will subside on its own. Excessive loss of hair for other reasons must be treated. Excessive shedding leaves Bulldog hair on the furniture, on your clothes, in fact everywhere. And Bulldog hair is difficult to get off, because it sticks.

A small pumice stone (two by four inches) helps remove the dead hair during heavy shedding. Brush with the stone in the direction of the hair growth. Complete the grooming with a slicker brush (a brush with many fine, slanted wire teeth) or a grooming glove (a cloth glove with textured pads on the palm), both of which can be purchased at a pet supply store.

When the shedding is normal, a daily brushing with a slicker brush or grooming glove should be adequate. Loose hair, dandruff, and dirt will be removed, leaving the coat bright and shiny and the hair follicles stimulated.

Even dogs with short coats need to be brushed. Brushing will keep your dog's coat healthy and cut down on shedding.

New Products in the Fight Against Fleas

At one time, battling fleas meant exposing your dog and your-self to toxic dips, sprays, powders, and collars. But today there are flea preventives that work very well and are safe for your dog, you, and the environment. The two most common types are insect growth regulators (IGRs), which stop the immature flea from developing or maturing, and adult flea killers. To deal with an active infestation, experts usually recommend a prod-uct that has both.

These next-generation flea fighters generally come in one of two forms:

- **Topical treatments or spot-ons.** These products are applied to the skin, usually between the shoulder blades. The product is absorbed through the skin into the dog's system.
- **Systemic products.** This is a pill your dog swallows that transmits a chemical throughout the dog's bloodstream. When a flea bites the dog, it picks up this chemical, which then prevents the flea's eggs from developing.

Talk to your veterinarian about which product is best for your dog. Make sure you read all the labels and apply the products exactly as recommended, and that you check to make sure they are safe for puppies.

Ears

Check the ears next. Observe the insides of the ears and look for dirt, excess wax, or any redness that might indicate an infection. A healthy ear will have a damp smell, while an infected ear will have a bad odor.

To clean the ears, fold one ear flap up over the dog's head so that the ear flap rests on his head. Dampen a cotton ball with witch hazel and, using your finger, gently swab out the ear, getting the cotton ball into all the cracks and crevices

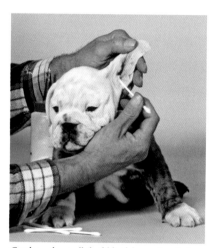

Gently swab out all the folds of the ear, but don't stick anything down into the ear canal.

of the ear. Do not reach into the ear canal. You may want to use two or three cotton balls per ear, especially if the ear is dirty. Leave the ear flap up for a moment or two so that the ear can dry. Then repeat on the other ear.

Eyes

If your Bulldog's eyes have some matter at the inside corners, just wipe them gently with a clean, damp cloth. If there is a continuing problem with excessive tearing or swollen lids, the lids may be turned in, a condition called *entropion*. In these situations, the eyelashes are rubbing against the surface of the eye, and this may require surgical intervention. See your veterinarian if you suspect this might be the case.

Those Hard-to-Reach Places

The Bulldog's wrinkle-covered face is certainly his trademark. But this is a trademark that requires daily care to keep the dog comfortable. Use mild soap (a soap you would use on your own face), warm water, and a soft cloth to wash between the wrinkles. Then dry the areas.

If your dog has a heavy nose wrinkle, lift it carefully and wash underneath, rinse, and dry. If it is especially dirty and inflamed, treat it with a medicated powder, baby powder, or cornstarch. It may be necessary to wash the wrinkles more than once a day. Use care and caution with powder. Be sure not to get any into the dog's eyes or nose and be sure it does not contain poisonous substances.

While you are cleaning the wrinkles on the dog's face, there are two more areas that must be cleaned. Most breeds of dogs care for their own personal hygiene by licking themselves. The Bulldog's stocky body makes it impossible for most Bulldogs to lick their private parts.

The female cannot reach her vulva to keep it clean. So after all the wrinkles are washed, wash Lady Bulldog's private parts, rinse, dry, and powder if inflamed. If there is inflammation, watch closely for discharge or odor. If this persists, a visit to the veterinarian is in order.

Mr. Bulldog cannot take care of his own personal hygiene, either, so check the inside of his hind legs. If there is evidence of dirt or discharge, wash thoroughly

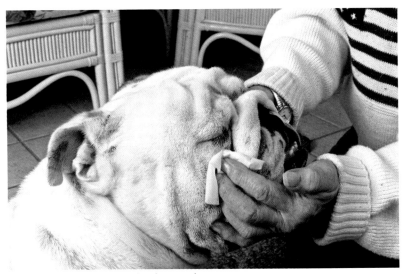

You'll have to wash and dry your dog's face every day.

with soap and water, rinse, and dry. As with the female, if inflammation is present or a discharge has a foul odor, have your veterinarian check his condition.

Finally, one more area is a Bulldog problem. If his tail is tight to his body, twisted and curled almost in knots, or is totally absent, then regular inspection and cleansing is the order of the day. Cover your finger with a soft, warm, soapy cloth and get under the tail. You will discover there is loose hair and flaking skin and other debris under the tail where it emerges from the body. Cleanse carefully and gently—dry and powder using whatever you used for wrinkles. Follow this same procedure in the knots and twists. If there is no tail, there is usually an indentation where the tail should be. This indentation will contain dead hair, dandruff, and other matter. This, too, must be cleaned.

Keeping this area clean and dry will help to prevent infection. A severely infected tail may have to be removed, which is expensive and painful. Prevention may be a nuisance, but it is less expensive for you, and certainly less painful for the dog, than treating an infection.

Bath Time

Bulldogs do not need frequent baths, but instead need bathing when they are dirty. Frequent brushing will do much more for a healthy, shiny coat than bathing.

Many Bulldogs actually enjoy bath time.

Most Bulldogs really enjoy a bath, though. If your dog is introduced to bathing when he is a puppy and is allowed to have fun during the process, he will enjoy the bath throughout his life.

Use baby shampoo or a shampoo made for dogs. A dog's skin is more sensitive than yours, so do not use harsh shampoo, medicated shampoo, or flea shampoo unless directed by your veterinarian. Be careful, and avoid getting shampoo in his eyes, ears, or nose. Wash his face as you do each morning and bathe the rest of the dog starting at the shoulders and going to the tail. Rinse well.

Let the dog shake off the water, then lift him out of the tub and finish drying him off with a towel. I don't like using a hair dryer, because the heat tends to dry the coat.

Get your puppy used to nail clipping early on and he won't make a big fuss about it.

How to Get Rid of a Tick

Although many of the new generation of flea fighters are partially effective in killing ticks once they are on your dog, they are not 100 percent effective and will not keep ticks from biting your dog in the first place. During tick season (which, depending on where you live, can be spring, summer, and/or fall), examine your dog every day for ticks. Pay particular attention to your dog's neck, behind the ears, the armpits, and the groin.

When you find a tick, use a pair of tweezers to grasp the tick as close as possible to the dog's skin and pull it out using firm, steady pressure. Check to make sure you get the whole tick (mouth parts left in your dog's skin can cause an infection), then wash the wound and dab it with a little antibiotic ointment. Watch for signs of inflammation.

Ticks carry very serious diseases that are transmittable to humans, so dispose of the tick safely. *Never* crush it between your fingers. Don't flush it down the toilet either, because the tick will survive the trip and infect another animal. Instead, use the tweezers to place the tick in a tight-sealing jar or plastic dish with a little alcohol, put on the lid, and dispose of the container in an outdoor garbage can. Wash the tweezers thoroughly with hot water and alcohol.

Toenails

All dogs living the modern cultured, domestic, protected existence must have their nails trimmed. Nail trimming should begin almost immediately after birth. At least every week the tip of the nail should be trimmed.

The only problem is that Bulldogs' nails are black. Even the tips are black. Because of this, it will be hard to see the quick (the end of the blood supply to

Making Your Environment Flea Free

If there are fleas on your dog, there are fleas in your home, yard, and car, even if you can't see them. Take these steps to combat them.

In your home:

- Wash whatever is washable (the dog bed, sheets, blankets, pillow covers, slipcovers, curtains, etc.).
- Vacuum everything else in your home—furniture, floors, rugs, everything. Pay special attention to the folds and crevices in upholstery, the cracks between floorboards, and the spaces between the floor and the baseboards. Flea larvae are sensitive to sunlight, so inside the house they prefer deep carpet, bedding, and cracks and crevices.
- When you're done, throw the vacuum cleaner bag away—in an outside garbage can.
- Use a nontoxic flea-killing powder to treat your carpets (but remember, it does not control fleas elsewhere in the house). The powder stays deep in the carpet and kills fleas (using a form of boric acid) for up to a year.
- If you have a particularly serious flea problem, consider using a fogger or long-lasting spray to kill any adult and larval fleas, or having a professional exterminator treat your home.

the nail). If you cut the quick, you'll hurt your dog and the nail may bleed. The best thing to do, then, is remove just the tips and clip more frequently.

For clipping, you will need a nail scissors or a guillotine type clipper, or you can buy an electric grinder. The grinder takes more time, but if the dog is cooperative, there is less danger of grinding the nail too short.

Start as soon as you get your puppy. At first, trim just the very tips so you do not cause any pain. If you are lucky, the dog will accept this procedure reluctantly. But you can get it done. I've only had one dog who would present his paws to have his nails trimmed.

If you cannot trim the nails, then either your veterinarian or a professional groomer should do it. You *must* keep nails trimmed or your dog's feet will become misshapen. A daily *long* walk on a rough surface (sidewalks work well) will make nail trimming necessary less often.

In your car:

- Take out the floor mats and hose them down with a strong stream of water, then hang them up to dry in the sun.
- Wash any towels, blankets, or other bedding you regularly keep in the car.
- Thoroughly vacuum the entire interior of your car, paying special attention to the seams between the bottom and back of the seats.
- When you're done, throw the vacuum cleaner bag away—in an outside garbage can.

In your yard:

- Flea larvae prefer shaded areas that have plenty of organic material and moisture, so rake the yard thoroughly and bag all the debris in tightly sealed bags.
- Spray your yard with an insecticide that has residual activity for at least thirty days. Insecticides that use a form of boric acid are nontoxic. Some products contain an insect growth regulator (such as fenoxycarb) and need to be applied only once or twice a year.
- For an especially difficult flea problem, consider having an exterminator treat your yard.
- Keep your yard free of piles of leaves, weeds, and other organic debris. Be especially careful in shady, moist areas, such as under bushes.

Mouth and Gums

If you start when your Bulldog is a puppy, keeping his teeth clean can be easy. Take some gauze from your first-aid kit and wrap it around your index finger. Dampen it and dip it in baking soda. With your Bulldog on his back in your lap, take that baking soda and rub it over your dog's teeth, working gently over each tooth, the inside and the outside, and into the gum line, taking care not to hurt the dog. Talk to him as you rub and praise him for his cooperation.

The rubbing action of the rough gauze and the chemical characteristics of the baking soda will help prevent plaque formation and will get rid of the bacteria that form on the teeth and gums.

Do two or three teeth and let your dog have a drink. Then work on a couple more. You may even want to break it into several sessions, doing half or a quarter of the dog's mouth at each session.

Chapter 8

Keeping Your Bulldog Healthy

The first step to having a healthy Bulldog is to get a healthy puppy, born of healthy parents. The next step is to find a good veterinarian. Choose a veterinarian *before* you bring your puppy home (see chapter 5 for information on choosing a veterinarian).

Set up an appointment with the veterinarian within seventy-two hours after you bring your new Bulldog home. Take all the information the breeder had given you (immunizations, worm checks, diet) so that your vet can evaluate it and make a plan for your dog's regular care. All this information will help the veterinarian establish a schedule to prevent problems rather than treat problems after they develop.

Internal Parasites

Parasites such as fleas and ticks that live on the outside of your Bulldog's body were discussed in chapter 7. Internal parasites can be a little more serious, because you can't see the problem and you may not even see any signs of an infestation until it has progressed.

Ascarids (Roundworms)

These long, white worms are common, especially in puppies, although they occasionally infest adult dogs and people. The adult female roundworm can lay

Most puppies have worms. It's not serious—if you treat them promptly.

up to 200,000 eggs a day, which are passed in the dog's feces. Roundworms are transmitted only via the feces. Because of this, stools should be picked up daily and your dog should be prevented from investigating other dogs' feces.

If treated early, roundworms are not serious. However, a heavy infestation can severely affect a dog's health. Puppies with roundworms will not thrive and will appear thin with a dull coat and a pot belly.

In people, roundworms can be more serious. Therefore, early treatment, regular fecal checks, and good sanitation are important, both for your Bulldog's continued good health and yours.

Giardia

This protozoal disease infects mammals and birds. The parasites live in the small intestines and are acquired when cysts are ingested from contaminated water.

Giardia is common in wild animals in many areas, so be careful if you take your Bulldog walking in the wilderness. If she drinks out of the local spring or stream, she can pick up giardia, just as you can. Diarrhea is one of the first signs. If your dog has diarrhea and you and your dog have been out in the wilds, make sure you tell your veterinarian.

Vaccines

What vaccines dogs need and how often they need them has been a subject of controversy for several years. Researchers, health care professionals, vaccine manufacturers, and dog owners do not always agree on which vaccines each dog needs or how often booster shots must be given.

In 2006, the American Animal Hospital Association issued a set of vaccination guidelines and recommendations intended to help dog owners and veterinarians sort through much of the controversy and conflicting information. The guidelines designate four vaccines as core, or essential for every dog, because of the serious nature of the diseases and their widespread distribution. These are canine distemper virus (using a modified live virus or recombinant modified live virus vaccine), canine parvovirus (using a modified live virus vaccine), canine adenovirus-2 (using a modified live virus vaccine), and rabies (using a killed virus). The general recommendations for their administration (except rabies, for which you must follow local laws) are:

- Vaccinate puppies at 6–8 weeks, 9–11 weeks, and 12–14 weeks.
- Give an initial "adult" vaccination when the dog is older than 16 weeks; two doses, three to four weeks apart, are

Heartworms

Adult heartworms live in the upper heart and greater pulmonary arteries, where they damage the vessel walls. Poor circulation is the result, which damages other bodily functions, eventually causing death from heart failure.

The adult worms produce thousands of tiny larvae called microfilaria. These circulate throughout the bloodstream until they are sucked up by an intermediate host, a mosquito. The microfilaria go through the larval stages in the mosquito, and then are transferred back to another dog when the mosquito bites again.

advised, but one dose is considered protective and acceptable.

- Give a booster shot when the dog is 1 year old.
- Give a subsequent booster shot every three years, unless there are risk factors that make it necessary to vaccinate more or less often.

Noncore vaccines should only be considered for those dogs who risk exposure to a particular disease because of geographic area, lifestyle, frequency of travel, or other issues. They include vaccines against distemper-measles virus, canine parainfluenza virus, leptospirosis, Bordetella bronchiseptica, and Borrelia burgdorferi (Lyme disease).

Vaccines that are not generally recommended because the disease poses little risk to dogs or is easily treatable, or the vaccine has not been proven to be effective, are those against giardia, canine coronavirus, and canine adenovirus-1.

Often, combination injections are given to puppies, with one shot containing several core and noncore vaccines. Your veterinarian may be reluctant to use separate shots that do not include the noncore vaccines, because they must be specially ordered. If you are concerned about these noncore vaccines, talk to your vet.

Dogs infected with heartworms can be treated if caught early. Unfortunately, the treatment itself can be risky and has killed some dogs. However, preventive medications are available that kill the larvae.

Heartworm infestation can be diagnosed by a blood test, and a negative result is required before starting the preventive.

Hookworms

Hookworms live their adult lives in the small intestines of dogs and other animals. They attach to the intestinal wall and suck blood. When they detach and move to a new location, the old wound continues to bleed because of the anti-coagulant the worm injects when it bites. Because of this, bloody diarrhea is usually the first sign of a problem.

Hookworm eggs are passed through the feces. Either they are picked up from the stools, as with roundworms, or, if conditions are right, they hatch in the soil and attach themselves to the feet of their new hosts, where they can burrow through the skin. They then migrate to the intestinal tract, where the cycle starts all over again.

People can pick up hookworms by walking barefoot in infected soil. In the Sunbelt states, children often pick up hookworm eggs when playing outside in the dirt or in a sandbox. Treatment, for both dogs and people, may have to be repeated.

Tapeworms

Tapeworms attach to the intestinal wall to absorb nutrients. They grow by creating new segments, and usually the first sign of an infestation is the ricelike segments found in the stools or on the dog's coat near the rectum. Tapeworms are acquired when the dog chews a flea bite and swallows a flea, the intermediate host. Therefore, a good flea-control program is the best way to prevent a tapeworm infestation.

Whipworms

Adult whipworms live in the large intestines, where they feed on blood. The eggs are passed in the stool and can live in the soil for many years. If your dog eats the fresh spring grass or buries her bone in the yard, she can pick up whipworm eggs from the infected soil. If you garden, you can pick up eggs under your fingernails, infecting yourself if you touch your face.

Heavy infestations cause diarrhea, often watery or bloody. The dog may appear thin and anemic, with a poor coat. Severe bowel problems may result. Unfortunately, whipworms can be difficult to detect, because the worms do not continually shed eggs. Therefore, a stool sample may be clear one day and show eggs the next day.

Any place that has mosquitoes has heartworms. Preventing them is far easier than treating an infestation.

Spaying and Neutering Your Bulldog

It's an old wives' tale that female dogs must have a litter of puppies to develop and mature properly. Bulldogs who are spayed will develop to the full extent of their genetic heritage.

In addition, raising Bulldogs is not for the faint of heart. Bulldogs, because of their large head, are rarely able to give birth naturally. Cesarean sections are the rule, not the exception, and as with any major surgery, this carries some risk. Many a Bulldog breeder has had to hand-raise a litter of puppies because the mother dog either did not survive the surgery or refused to care for her puppies after the surgery.

Some research scientists believe the trauma of the heat cycle is almost as great as pregnancy and puppies. In this case, it is only fair that your female be relieved of this biannual bodily function by being spayed as early as possible.

Most veterinarians advise spaying before the first heat period. Discuss the options with your vet as soon as possible. There is some risk in spaying, but the risk is minimal when compared to the risks involved with pregnancy and birth, as well as the risks of cancer, pyometra, and unwanted pregnancy in an unspayed female.

Male dogs can be neutered at any point after about 4 months of age although many shelters are doing it as early as 8 to 10 weeks of age. Talk to your veterinarian and ask about the best time to neuter your male Bulldog.

Neutered males are less likely to provoke fights with other males, are less likely to look for ways out of the yard to go find a female, and develop fewer bad habits that are caused by hormones. In addition, testicular cancer and other diseases of the reproductive system are prevented when you have your dog neutered.

> **TIP**
>
> Forget trying to make money by breeding your dog, especially your Bulldog. Artificial insemination, cesarean sections, special food, equipment, time, and other requirements make breeding a very expensive venture.

Common Health Problems

Your Bulldog may never come down with any of these problems, but it's a good idea to be aware of them just in case. If, at any time, your feel your dog is sick, call your veterinarian for guidance.

Why Spay and Neuter?

Breeding dogs is a serious undertaking that should only be part of a well-planned breeding program. Why? Because dogs pass on their physical and behavioral problems to their offspring. Even healthy, well-behaved dogs can pass on problems in their genes.

Is your dog so sweet that you'd like to have a litter of puppies just like her? If you breed her to another dog, the pups will not have the same genetic heritage she has. Breeding her *parents* again will increase the odds of a similar pup, but even then, the puppies in the second litter could inherit different genes. In fact, *there is no way to breed a dog to be just like another dog.*

Meanwhile, thousands and thousands of dogs are killed in animal shelters every year simply because they have no homes. Casual breeding is a big contributor to this problem.

If you don't plan to breed your dog, is it still a good idea to spay her or neuter him? Yes!

When you spay your female:

- You avoid her heat cycles, during which she discharges blood and scent.
- It greatly reduces the risk of mammary cancer and eliminates the risk of pyometra (an often fatal infection of the uterus) and uterine cancer.
- It prevents unwanted pregnancies.
- It reduces dominance behaviors and aggression.

When you neuter your male:

- It curbs the desire to roam and to fight with other males.
- It greatly reduces the risk of prostate cancer and eliminates the risk of testicular cancer.
- It helps reduce leg lifting and mounting behavior.
- It reduces dominance behaviors and aggression.

Your dog is relying on you to know when to call the veterinarian, so familiarize yourself with common canine health issues.

Animal Bites

If your dog has been bitten by a dog or another animal, clean the wound with soap and water (preferably with an antiseptic scrub) and call your veterinarian. Check the status of your dog's rabies vaccination, as well.

Bee Stings and Spider Bites

Some dogs are allergic to these bites. Quick treatment is required if the dog's head, face, and feet begin swelling and respiration becomes labored. You can give your dog Benadryl (an antihistamine). Give two 25-mg tablets for a fifty-pound dog. Then call your veterinarian right away.

Bleeding

Apply pressure and an ice bag to the site of the bleeding. The extent of the injury and the amount of bleeding are the criteria for the need for speed and professional treatment. If the blood is spurting, put pressure on it and call your veterinarian immediately for guidance. Never put on a tourniquet unless told to by your veterinarian, as this could result in the loss of the limb.

Vomiting blood, blood in the urine, and rectal bleeding all require an accurate diagnosis before treatment can begin. Take your dog to the veterinarian right away.

Bloat and Torsion

When a dog bloats, the stomach enlarges. Although it often happens after the dog has eaten and then drunk some water (which causes the food to expand), it can also happen when gases in the food expand. If the stomach is greatly enlarged, it can twist or turn, cutting off any avenue for the food, water, and gases to escape from the stomach. This is called torsion.

A dog in the midst of bloat will pace or act restless, may bite or paw at the abdomen, may have a swollen abdomen, and may attempt to

Bulldogs with their big chests are among the breeds prone to bloat.

vomit. Bloat alone can be life threatening, and torsion definitely is; the dog will go into shock shortly after the stomach turns. Veterinary care is needed immediately!

Broken Bones

Support the bone that appears to be broken and take the dog immediately to the veterinarian. X-rays are usually necessary. What do you have about the house to use for a temporary splint? How about rolled-up newspapers, or a small, thin foam rubber pillow, or a wooden spatula or a ruler? Use your imagination and fasten the splint with adhesive tape, masking tape, or strips of old sheets, and take the dog to the veterinarian.

Choking

Reach into the dog's mouth and try to pull out whatever may be choking her. Pull her tongue out to clear an airway. If whatever caused her to choke has been removed, she will probably be all right. If she continues to try to vomit, then she must go to the veterinarian.

Diarrhea

How long has the diarrhea lasted? If it's just a one-time problem that does not recur in a day or two, you need not be alarmed. But if the stools are frequent for twenty-four hours or more, or contain blood, mucus, or undigested food, let the veterinarian make the diagnosis and prescribe the treatment. As time goes on, you will learn when to push the panic button and when to wait a little while.

Eye Injuries

If the dog has injured her eye or has something in the eye, wash it out with eyewash or warm tap water. Cover the eye if your dog is pawing or scratching at it. Prompt diagnosis and treatment by your veterinarian may prevent corneal damage.

Overheating

Bulldogs cannot tolerate heat. If your dog stops walking or playing and plops down on the ground, is panting heavily, feels hot to the touch, and looks very stressed, bathe her feet and underside with cool water or put her in a tub of cool (not cold) water. If this is not possible, place small bags filled with ice under her front legs, in the groin, and on her head. Wrap her in towels that have been soaked in cool water. If possible, turn a fan on her. Keep her quiet.

Bulldogs cannot tolerate heat. In warm weather, always watch your dog for signs of overheating.

Do not give the dog ice chips or water unless she takes them willingly. As long as her gum color remains good (nice and pink; not pale pink or white) and her breathing is regular, she probably is not in grave danger. But this is your veterinarian's decision to make, so give the vet a call.

Poisoning

In every home there are cleaning fluids, fingernail polish, bleach, and other poisons. Few Bulldogs would eat or drink these things, but no Bulldog should have access to them. Store household necessities, fertilizers, insect sprays, and so on in secure cupboards and on high shelves.

Keep the poison control telephone number (see the box on page 90), your veterinarian's number, and the number of the nearest emergency vet clinic by your telephone. Call these experts for their advice. There are too many chemicals and too many complicated formulas for the average person to know what action to take in an emergency. Sometimes the animal should be made to vomit, sometimes she should have a gastric lavage (washing out of the stomach), and sometimes this action would be fatal. Only the professionals can evaluate the situation.

ASPCA Animal Poison Control Center

The ASPCA Animal Poison Control Center has a staff of licensed veterinarians and board-certified toxicologists available 24 hours a day, 365 days a year. The number to call is (888) 426-4435. You will be charged a consultation fee of $60 per case, charged to most major credit cards. There is no charge for follow-up calls in critical cases. At your request, they will also contact your veterinarian. Specific treatment and information can be provided via fax.

Keep the poison control number in large, legible print with your other emergency telephone numbers. When you call, be prepared to give your name, address, and phone number; what your dog has gotten into (the amount and how long ago); your dog's breed, age, sex, and weight; and what signs and symptoms the dog is showing. You can log onto www.aspca.org and click on "Animal Poison Control Center" for more information, including a list of toxic and nontoxic plants.

Vomiting

If your dog vomits just once, nothing needs to be done. However, if vomiting is persistent, or contains blood, mucus, or large amounts of undigested food, the veterinarian should be called. Your veterinarian will ask several questions, including, Did the dog get into the garbage, chew up a toy, or swallow a foreign substance? Does she have a fever? Take a good look at what your dog has vomited up so that you can answer those questions.

Problems Particular to Bulldogs

Most of this breed's health problems are due to their shortened muzzles and their inability to give birth naturally. Although their life span is only about ten to fifteen years, those years are relatively healthy and happy. Still, Bulldogs do occasionally suffer from conditions to which the breed seems to be predisposed. Of course, not all Bulldogs have these problems. But some do.

The Bulldog's shortened muzzle can cause some health problems.

Acne

When the Bulldog becomes a teenager (between 6 and 8 months of age), she may develop acne. Just as with human teenagers, this is due to hormonal changes in the body. Keep the dog's face and wrinkles clean. If the problem gets bad, talk to your veterinarian about prescribing medication. Do not use human acne medications without your veterinarian's recommendation.

Brachycephalic Difficulties

Like other breeds with shortened muzzles (such as Pugs and Pekingese), Bulldogs can have breathing difficulties, especially in

You can expect your Bulldog to live ten to fifteen years. Seniors will need extra TLC.

When to Call the Veterinarian

Go to the vet right away or take your dog to an emergency veterinary clinic if:

- Your dog is choking
- Your dog is having trouble breathing
- Your dog has been injured and you cannot stop the bleeding within a few minutes
- Your dog has been stung or bitten by an insect and the site is swelling
- Your dog has been bitten by a snake
- Your dog has been bitten by another animal (including a dog) and shows any swelling or bleeding
- Your dog has touched, licked, or in any way been exposed to poison
- Your dog has been burned by either heat or caustic chemicals
- Your dog has been hit by a car
- Your dog has any obvious broken bones or cannot put any weight on one of her limbs
- Your dog has a seizure

Make an appointment to see the vet as soon as possible if:

- Your dog has been bitten by a cat, another dog, or a wild animal
- Your dog has been injured and is still limping an hour later

hot, humid weather. If your dog ever has trouble breathing or her lips or mucus membranes turn blue, call your veterinarian immediately. This may be a temporary problem, but it may also be life threatening.

Elongated Soft Palate

The soft palate is the flap of skin at the back of the throat. Loud, noisy, or difficult breathing may indicate an elongated soft palate—a common breathing disorder in all brachycephalic (short-muzzled) breeds.

- Your dog has unexplained swelling or redness
- Your dog's appetite changes
- Your dog vomits repeatedly and can't seem to keep food down, or drools excessively while eating
- You see any changes in your dog's urination or defecation (pain during elimination, change in regular habits, blood in urine or stool, diarrhea, foul-smelling stool)
- Your dog scoots her rear end on the floor
- Your dog's energy level, attitude, or behavior changes for no apparent reason
- Your dog has crusty or cloudy eyes, or excessive tearing or discharge
- Your dog's nose is dry or chapped, hot, crusty, or runny
- Your dog's ears smell foul, have a dark discharge, or seem excessively waxy
- Your dog's gums are inflamed or bleeding, her teeth look brown, or her breath is foul
- Your dog's skin is red, flaky, itchy, or inflamed, or she keeps chewing at certain spots
- Your dog's coat is dull, dry, brittle, or bare in spots
- Your dog's paws are red, swollen, tender, cracked, or the nails are split or too long
- Your dog is panting excessively, wheezing, unable to catch her breath, breathing heavily, or sounds strange when she breathes

In dogs with this condition, the skin and tissue on the roof of the mouth will either hang in front of the airway or will fall into the larynx when the dog inhales, causing the skin to vibrate or partially block the airways. It can impede breathing. The dog can also choke on or spit up pieces of kibble and even pass out from a lack of air.

Signs are excessive panting, being unable to calm down when excited, and possibly vomiting. Loud, raspy breathing when the dog is overheated is another sign.

This condition can be taken care of with minor surgery. This is a genetic defect, and dogs with this problem should not be bred.

How to Make a Canine First-Aid Kit

If your dog hurts herself, even a minor cut, it can be very upsetting for both of you. Having a first-aid kit handy will help you to help her, calmly and efficiently. What should be in your canine first-aid kit?

- Antibiotic ointment
- Antiseptic and antibacterial cleansing wipes
- Benadryl
- Cotton-tipped applicators
- Disposable razor
- Elastic wrap bandages
- Extra leash and collar
- First-aid tape of various widths
- Gauze bandage roll
- Gauze pads of different sizes, including eye pads
- Hydrogen peroxide
- Instant cold compress
- Kaopectate or Pepto-Bismol tablets or liquid
- Latex gloves
- Lubricating jelly
- Muzzle
- Nail clippers
- Pen, pencil, and paper for notes and directions
- Plastic syringe with no needle (for administering liquids)
- Round-ended scissors and pointy scissors
- Safety pins
- Sterile saline eyewash
- Thermometer (rectal)
- Tweezers

Entropion

Bulldogs, because of their short faces and wrinkles, may have entropion eyelids. Other short-muzzled breeds are subject to this same problem. This is a condition in which the eyelashes turn in and rub against the surface of the eye. The eyes will be inflamed, the lids swollen, and there is excessive tearing. It will irritate the eye and may cause blindness.

The treatment is a minor surgical procedure, or, if *very* minor, your veterinarian may be able to give you medication to put in the eye. But this is a daily chore, and a more permanent solution is surgical intervention. Entropion is a genetic defect, and dogs who are affected should not be bred.

Hip Dysplasia

Unfortunately Bulldogs, because of their build, may have dysplastic hips. Hip dysplasia is a failure of the head of the femur (thighbone) to fit properly into the acetabulum (hip socket). Hip dysplasia is not just caused by poorly formed or malpositioned bones; many researchers believe the muscles and tendons in the leg and hip may also play a part.

Hip dysplasia is considered to be a polygenic inherited disorder, which means many different genes may lead to the disease. Also, environmental factors may contribute to the development of hip dysplasia, including nutrition and exercise, although the part environmental factors play in the disease is highly debated among experts.

Whatever the cause or causes of this problem, hip dysplasia can cause a wide range of problems, from mild lameness to movement irregularities to crippling pain. Dogs with hip dysplasia must often limit their activities, may need corrective surgery, or may even need to be euthanized because of the pain.

Hypothyroidism

A high percentage of Bulldogs suffer from hypothyroidism (underactive thyroid). One of the most common signs is loss of hair on the animal's sides. If it's not treated, there will be complications, including hair loss, changes in the skin, lethargy, reproductive problems, and more.

Tests evaluating the thyroid function are becoming more accurate, and a tiny pill given daily will return the thyroid gland to its normal function.

Breeders can test their dogs for structural problems such as hip dysplasia, helping to reduce the incidence in the breed.

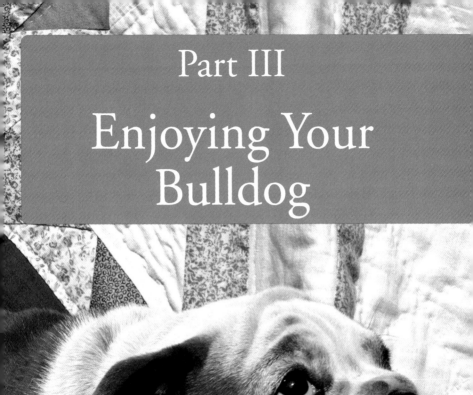

Part III
Enjoying Your Bulldog

Chapter 9

Training Your Bulldog

by Peggy Moran

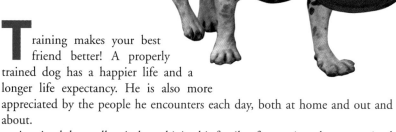

Training makes your best friend better! A properly trained dog has a happier life and a longer life expectancy. He is also more appreciated by the people he encounters each day, both at home and out and about.

A trained dog walks nicely and joins his family often, going places untrained dogs cannot go. He is never rude or unruly, and he always happily comes when called. When he meets people for the first time, he greets them by sitting and waiting to be petted, rather than jumping up. At home he doesn't compete with his human family, and alone he is not destructive or overly anxious. He isn't continually nagged with words like "no," since he has learned not to misbehave in the first place. He is never shamed, harshly punished, or treated unkindly, and he is a well-loved, involved member of the family.

Sounds good, doesn't it? If you are willing to invest some time, thought, and patience, the words above could soon be used to describe your dog (though perhaps changing "he" to "she"). Educating your pet in a positive way is fun and easy, and there is no better gift you can give your pet than the guarantee of improved understanding and a great relationship.

This chapter will explain how to offer kind leadership, reshape your pet's behavior in a positive and practical way, and even get a head start on simple obedience training.

Understanding Builds the Bond

Dog training is a learning adventure on both ends of the leash. Before attempting to teach their dog new behaviors or change unwanted ones, thoughtful dog owners take the time to understand why their pets behave the way they do, and how their own behavior can be either a positive or negative influence on their dog.

Canine Nature

Loving dogs as much as we do, it's easy to forget they are a completely different species. Despite sharing our homes and living as appreciated members of our families, dogs do not think or learn exactly the same way people do. Even if you love your dog like a child, you must remember to respect the fact that he is actually a dog.

Dogs have no idea when their behavior is inappropriate from a human perspective. They are not aware of the value of possessions they chew or of messes they make or the worry they sometimes seem to cause. While people tend to look at behavior as good and bad or right and wrong, dogs just discover what works and what doesn't work. Then they behave accordingly, learning from their own experiences and increasing or reducing behaviors to improve results for themselves.

You might wonder, "But don't dogs want to please us?" My answer is yes, provided your pleasure reflects back to them in positive ways they can feel and appreciate. Dogs do things for *dog* reasons, and everything they do works for them in some way or they wouldn't be doing it!

The Social Dog

Our pets descended from animals who lived in tightly knit, cooperative social groups. Though far removed in appearance and lifestyle from their ancestors, our dogs still relate in many of the same ways their wild relatives did. And in their relationships with one another, wild canids either lead or follow.

Canine ranking relationships are not about cruelty and power; they are about achievement and abilities. Competent dogs with high levels of drive and confidence step up, while deferring dogs step aside. But followers don't get the short end of the stick; they benefit from the security of having a more competent dog at the helm.

Our domestic dogs still measure themselves against other members of their group—us! Dog owners whose actions lead to positive results have willing, secure followers. But dogs may step up and fill the void or cut loose and do their own thing when their people fail to show capable leadership. When dogs are pushy, aggressive, and rude, or independent and unwilling, it's not because they have designs on the role of "master." It is more likely their owners failed to provide consistent leadership.

Dogs in training benefit from their handler's good leadership. Their education flows smoothly because they are impressed. Being in charge doesn't require you to physically dominate or punish your dog. You simply need to make some subtle changes in the way you relate to him every day.

Lead Your Pack!

Create schedules and structure daily activities. Dogs are creatures of habit and routines will create security. Feed meals at the same times each day and also try to schedule regular walks, training practices, and toilet outings. Your predictability will help your dog be patient.

Ask your dog to perform a task. Before releasing him to food or freedom, have him do something as simple as sit on command. Teach him that cooperation earns great results!

Give a release prompt (such as "let's go") when going through doors leading outside. This is a better idea than allowing your impatient pup to rush past you.

Pet your dog when he is calm, not when he is excited. Turn your touch into a tool that relaxes and settles.

Reward desirable rather than inappropriate behavior. Petting a jumping dog (who hasn't been invited up) reinforces jumping. Pet sitting dogs, and only invite lap dogs up after they've first "asked" by waiting for your invitation.

Replace personal punishment with positive reinforcement. Show a dog what *to do,* and motivate him to want to do it, and there will be no need to punish him for what he should *not do.* Dogs naturally follow, without the need for force or harshness.

Play creatively and appropriately. Your dog will learn the most about his social rank when he is playing with you. During play, dogs work to control toys and try to get the best of one another in a friendly way. The wrong sorts of play can create problems: For example, tug of war can lead to aggressiveness. Allowing your dog to control toys during play may result in possessive guarding when he has something he really values, such as a bone. Dogs who are chased during play may later run away from you when you approach to leash them. The right kinds of play will help increase your dog's social confidence while you gently assert your leadership.

How Dogs Learn (and How They Don't)

Dog training begins as a meeting of minds—yours and your dog's. Though the end goal may be to get your dog's body to behave in a specific way, training starts as a mind game. Your dog is learning all the time by observing the consequences of his actions and social interactions. He is always seeking out what he perceives as desirable and trying to avoid what he perceives as undesirable.

He will naturally repeat a behavior that either brings him more good stuff or makes bad stuff go away (these are both types of reinforcement). He will naturally avoid a behavior that brings him more bad stuff or makes the good stuff go away (these are both types of punishment).

Both reinforcement and punishment can be perceived as either the direct result of something the dog did himself, or as coming from an outside source.

Using Life's Rewards

Your best friend is smart and he is also cooperative. When the best things in life can only be had by working with you, your dog will view you as a facilitator. You unlock doors to all of the positively reinforcing experiences he values: his freedom, his friends at the park, food, affection, walks, and play. The trained dog accompanies you through those doors and waits to see what working with you will bring.

Rewarding your dog for good behavior is called positive reinforcement, and, as we've just seen, it increases the likelihood that he will repeat that behavior. The perfect reward is anything your dog wants that is safe and appropriate. Don't limit yourself to toys, treats, and things that come directly from you. Harness life's positives—barking at squirrels, chasing a falling leaf, bounding away from you at the dog park, pausing for a moment to sniff everything—and allow your dog to earn access to those things as rewards that come from cooperating with you. When he looks at you, when he sits, when he comes when you call—any prompted behavior can earn one of life's rewards. When he works with you, he earns the things he most appreciates; but when he tries to get those things on his own, he cannot. Rather than seeing you as someone who always says "no," your dog will view you as the one who says "let's go!" He will *want* to follow.

What About Punishment?

Not only is it unnecessary to personally punish dogs, it is abusive. No matter how convinced you are that your dog "knows right from wrong," in reality he will associate personal punishment with the punisher. The resulting cowering, "guilty"-looking postures are actually displays of submission and fear. Later,

---

Purely Positive Reinforcement

With positive training, we emphasize teaching dogs what they should do to earn reinforcements, rather than punishing them for unwanted behaviors.

- Focus on teaching "do" rather than "don't." For example, a sitting dog isn't jumping.
- Use positive reinforcers that are valuable to your dog and the situation: A tired dog values rest; a confined dog values freedom.
- Play (appropriately)!
- Be a consistent leader.
- Set your dog up for success by anticipating and preventing problems.
- Notice and reward desirable behavior, and give him lots of attention when he is being good.
- Train ethically. Use humane methods and equipment that do not frighten or hurt your dog.
- When you are angry, walk away and plan a positive strategy.
- Keep practice sessions short and sweet. Five to ten minutes, three to five times a day is best.

---

when the punisher isn't around and the coast is clear, the same behavior he was punished for—such as raiding a trash can—might bring a self-delivered, very tasty result. The punished dog hasn't learned not to misbehave; he has learned to not get caught.

Does punishment ever have a place in dog training? Many people will heartily insist it does not. But dog owners often get frustrated as they try to stick to the path of all-positive reinforcement. It sure sounds great, but is it realistic, or even natural, to *never* say "no" to your dog?

A wild dog's life is not *all* positive. Hunger and thirst are both examples of negative reinforcement; the resulting discomfort motivates the wild dog to seek food and water. He encounters natural aversives such as pesky insects; mats in his coat; cold days; rainy days; sweltering hot days; and occasional run-ins with thorns, brambles, skunks, bees, and other nastiness. These all affect his behavior, as he tries to avoid the bad stuff whenever possible. The wild dog also occasionally encounters social punishers from others in his group when he gets too pushy. Starting with a growl or a snap from Mom, and later some mild and ritualized discipline from other members of his four-legged family, he learns to modify behaviors that elicit grouchy responses.

Our pet dogs don't naturally experience all positive results either, because they learn from their surroundings and from social experiences with other dogs. Watch a group of pet dogs playing together and you'll see a very old educational system still being used. As they wrestle and attempt to assert themselves, you'll notice many mouth-on-neck moments. Their playful biting is inhibited, with no intention to cause harm, but their message is clear: "Say uncle or this could hurt more!"

Observing that punishment does occur in nature, some people may feel compelled to try to be like the big wolf with their pet dogs. Becoming aggressive or heavy-handed with your pet will backfire! Your dog will not be impressed, nor will he want to follow you. Punishment causes dogs to change their behavior to avoid or escape discomfort and threats. Threatened dogs will either become very passive and offer submissive, appeasing postures, attempt to flee, or rise to the occasion and fight back. When people personally punish their dogs in an angry manner, one of these three defensive mechanisms will be triggered. Which one depends on a dog's genetic temperament as well as his past social experiences. Since we don't want to make our pets feel the need to avoid or escape us, personal punishment has no place in our training.

Remote Consequences

Sometimes, however, all-positive reinforcement is just not enough. That's because not all reinforcement comes from us. An inappropriate behavior can be self-reinforcing—just doing it makes the dog feel better in some way, whether you are there to say "good boy!" or not. Some examples are eating garbage, pulling the stuffing out of your sofa, barking at passersby, or urinating on the floor.

Although you don't want to personally punish your dog, the occasional deterrent may be called for to help derail these kinds of self-rewarding misbehaviors. In these cases, mild forms of impersonal or remote punishment can be used as part of a correction. The goal isn't to make your dog feel bad or to "know he has done wrong," but to help redirect him to alternate behaviors that are more acceptable to you.

The Problems with Personal Punishment

- Personally punished dogs are not taught appropriate behaviors.
- Personally punished dogs only stop misbehaving when they are caught or interrupted, but they don't learn not to misbehave when they are alone.
- Personally punished dogs become shy, fearful, and distrusting.
- Personally punished dogs may become defensively aggressive.
- Personally punished dogs become suppressed and inhibited.
- Personally punished dogs become stressed, triggering stress-reducing behaviors that their owners interpret as acts of spite, triggering even more punishment.
- Personally punished dogs have stressed owners.
- Personally punished dogs may begin to repeat behaviors they have been taught will result in negative, but predictable, attention.
- Personally punished dogs are more likely to be given away than are positively trained dogs.

You do this by pairing a slightly startling, totally impersonal sound with an equally impersonal and *very mild* remote consequence. The impersonal sound might be a single shake of an empty plastic pop bottle with pennies in it, held out of your dog's sight. Or you could use a vocal expression such as "eh!" delivered with you looking *away* from your misbehaving dog.

Pair your chosen sound—the penny bottle or "eh!"—with either a slight tug on his collar or a sneaky spritz on the rump from a water bottle. Do this right *as* he touches something he should not; bad timing will confuse your dog and undermine your training success.

To keep things under your control and make sure you get the timing right, it's best to do this as a setup. "Accidentally" drop a shoe on the floor, and then help your dog learn some things are best avoided. As he sniffs the shoe say "eh!" without looking at him and give a *slight* tug against his collar. This sound will quickly become meaningful as a correction all by itself—sometimes after just one setup—making the tug correction obsolete. The tug lets your dog see that you were right; going for that shoe *was* a bad idea! Your wise dog will be more likely to heed your warning next time, and probably move closer to you where it's safe. Be a good friend and pick up the nasty shoe. He'll be relieved and you'll look heroic. Later, when he's home alone and encounters a stray shoe, he'll want to give it a wide berth.

Your negative marking sound will come in handy in the future, when your dog begins to venture down the wrong behavioral path. The goal is not to announce your disapproval or to threaten your dog. You are not telling him to stop or showing how *you* feel about his behavior. You are sounding a warning to a friend who's venturing off toward danger—"I wouldn't if I were you!" Suddenly, there is an abrupt, rather startling, noise! Now is the moment to redirect him and help him earn positive reinforcement. That interrupted behavior will become something he wants to avoid in the future, but he won't want to avoid you.

Practical Commands for Family Pets

Before you begin training your dog, let's look at some equipment you'll want to have on hand:

- **A buckle collar** is fine for most dogs. If your dog pulls *very* hard, try a head collar, a device similar to a horse halter that helps reduce pulling by turning the dog's head. *Do not* use a choke chain (sometimes called a training collar), because they cause physical harm even when used correctly.
- **Six-foot training leash and twenty-six–foot retractable leash.**
- **A few empty plastic soda bottles with about twenty pennies in each one.** This will be used to impersonally interrupt misbehaviors before redirecting dogs to more positive activities.
- **A favorite squeaky toy,** to motivate, attract attention, and reward your dog during training.

Lure your dog to take just a few steps with you on the leash by being inviting and enthusiastic. Make sure you reward him for his efforts.

Baby Steps

Allow your young pup to drag a short, lightweight leash attached to a buckle collar for a few *supervised* moments, several times each day. At first the leash may annoy him and he may jump around a bit trying to get away from it. Distract him with your squeaky toy or a bit of his kibble and he'll quickly get used to his new "tail."

Begin walking him on the leash by holding the end and following him. As he adapts, you can begin to assert gentle direct pressure to teach him to follow you. Don't jerk or yank, or he will become afraid to walk when the leash is on. If he becomes hesitant, squat down facing him and let him figure out that by moving toward you he is safe and secure. If he remains confused or frightened and doesn't come to you, go to him and help him understand that you provide safe harbor while he's on the leash. Then back away a few steps and try again to lure him to you. As he learns that you are the "home base," he'll want to follow when you walk a few steps, waiting for you to stop, squat down, and make him feel great.

So Attached to You!

The next step in training your dog—and this is a very important one—is to begin spending at least an hour or more each day with him on a four- to six-foot leash, held by or tethered to you. This training will increase his attachment to you—literally!—as you sit quietly or walk about, tending to your household business. When you are quiet, he'll learn it is time to settle; when you are active, he'll learn to move with you. Tethering also keeps him out of trouble when you are busy but still want his company. It is a great alternative to confining a dog, and can be used instead of crating any time you're home and need to slow him down a bit.

Rotating your dog from supervised freedom to tethered time to some quiet time in the crate or his gated area gives him a diverse and balanced day while he is learning. Two confined or tethered hours is the most you should require of your dog in one stretch, before changing to some supervised freedom, play, or a walk.

The dog in training may, at times, be stressed by all of the changes he is dealing with. Provide a stress outlet, such as a toy to chew on, when he is confined or tethered. He will settle into his quiet time more quickly and completely. Always be sure to provide several rounds of daily play and free time (in a fenced area or on your retractable leash) in addition to plenty of chewing materials.

Dog Talk

Dogs don't speak in words, but they do have a language—body language. They use postures, vocaliza-
tions, movements, facial gestures,

Tethering your dog is great way to keep him calm and under control, but still with you.

odors, and touch—usually with their mouths—to communicate what they are feeling and thinking.

We also "speak" using body language. We have quite an array of postures, movements, and facial gestures that accompany our touch and language as we attempt to communicate with our pets. And our dogs can quickly figure us out!

Alone, without associations, words are just noises. But, because we pair them with meaningful body language, our dogs make the connection. Dogs can really learn to understand much of what we *say*, if what we *do* at the same time is consistent.

The Positive Marker

Start your dog's education with one of the best tricks in dog training: Pair vari-
ous positive reinforcers—food, a toy, touch—with a sound such as a click on a clicker (which you can get at the pet supply store) or a spoken word like "good!" or "yes!" This will enable you to later "mark" your dog's desirable behaviors.

It seems too easy: Just say "yes!" and give the dog his toy. (Or use whatever sound and reward you have chosen.) Later, when you make your marking sound right at the instant your dog does the right thing, he will know you are going to be giving him something good for that particular action. And he'll be eager to repeat the behavior to hear you mark it again!

Next, you must teach your dog to understand the meaning of cues you'll be using to ask him to perform specific behaviors. This is easy, too. Does he already do things you might like him to do on command? Of course! He lies down, he sits, he picks things up, he drops them again, he comes to you. All of the behaviors you'd like to control are already part of your dog's natural repertoire. The trick is getting him to offer those behaviors when you ask for them. And that means you have to teach him to associate a particular behavior on his part with a particular behavior on your part.

Sit Happens

Teach your dog an important new rule: From now on, he is only touched and petted when he is either sitting or lying down. You won't need to ask him to sit; in fact, you should not. Just keep him tethered near you so there isn't much to do but stand, be ignored, or settle, and wait until sit happens.

He may pester you a bit, but be stoic and unresponsive. Starting now, when *you* are sitting down, a sitting dog is the only one you see and pay attention to. He will eventually sit, and as he does, attach the word "sit"—but don't be too excited or he'll jump right back up. Now mark with your positive sound that promises something good, then reward him with a slow, quiet, settling pet.

Training requires consistent reinforcement. Ask others to also wait until your dog is sitting and calm to touch him, and he will associate being petted with being relaxed. Be sure you train your dog to associate everyone's touch with quiet bonding.

Reinforcing "Sit" as a Command

Since your dog now understands one concept of working for a living—sit to earn petting—you can begin to shape and reinforce his desire to sit. Hold toys, treats, his bowl of food, and turn into a statue. But don't prompt him to sit! Instead, remain frozen and unavailable, looking somewhere out into space, over his head. He will put on a bit of a show, trying to get a response from you, and may offer various behaviors, but only one will push your button—sitting. Wait for him to offer the "right" behavior, and when he does, you unfreeze. Say "sit," then mark with an excited "good!" and give him the toy or treat with a release command—"OK!"

When you notice spontaneous sits occurring, be sure to take advantage of those free opportunities to make your command sequence meaningful and positive. Say "sit" as you observe sit happen—then mark with "good!" and praise, pet, or reward the dog. Soon, every time you look at your dog he'll be sitting and looking right back at you!

Now, after thirty days of purely positive practice, it's time to give him a test. When he is just walking around doing his own thing, suddenly ask him to sit. He'll probably do it right away. If he doesn't, do *not* repeat your command, or you'll just undermine its meaning ("sit" means sit *now;* the command is not "sit, sit, sit, sit"). Instead, get something he likes and let him know you have it. Wait for him to offer the sit—he will—then say "sit!" and complete your marking and rewarding sequence.

OK

"OK" will probably rate as one of your dog's favorite words. It's like the word "recess" to schoolchildren. It is the word used to release your dog from a command. You can introduce "OK" during your "sit" practice. When he gets up from a sit, say "OK" to tell him the sitting is finished. Soon that sound will mean "freedom."

Make it even more meaningful and positive. Whenever he spontaneously bounds away, say "OK!" Squeak a toy, and when he notices and shows interest, toss it for him.

Down

I've mentioned that you should only pet your dog when he is either sitting or lying down. Now, using the approach I've just introduced for "sit," teach your dog to lie down. You will be a statue, and hold something he would like to get but that you'll only release to a dog who is lying down. It helps to lower the desired item to the floor in front of him, still not speaking and not letting him have it until he offers you the new behavior you are seeking.

Lower your dog's reward to the floor to help him figure out what behavior will earn him his reward.

He may offer a sit and then wait expectantly, but you must make him keep searching for the new trick that triggers your generosity. Allow your dog to experiment and find the right answer, even if he has to search around for it first. When he lands on "down" and learns it is another behavior that works, he'll offer it more quickly the next time.

Don't say "down" until he lies down, to tightly associate your prompt with the correct behavior. To say "down, down, down" as he is sitting, looking at you, or pawing at the toy would make "down" mean those behaviors instead! Whichever behavior he offers, a training opportunity has been created. Once you've attached and shaped both sitting and lying down, you can ask for both behaviors with your verbal prompts, "sit" or "down." Be sure to only reinforce the "correct" reply!

Stay

"Stay" can easily be taught as an extension of what you've already been practicing. To teach "stay," you follow the entire sequence for reinforcing a "sit" or "down," except you wait a bit longer before you give the release word, "OK!" Wait a second or two longer during each practice before saying "OK!" and releasing your dog to the positive reinforcer (toy, treat, or one of life's other rewards).

You can step on the leash to help your dog understand the down-stay, but only do this when he is already lying down. You don't want to hurt him!

If he gets up before you've said "OK," you have two choices: pretend the release was your idea and quickly interject "OK!" as he breaks; or, if he is more experienced and practiced, mark the behavior with your correction sound—"eh!"— and then gently put him back on the spot, wait for him to lie down, and begin again. Be sure the next three practices are a success. Ask him to wait for just a second, and release him before he can be wrong. You need to keep your dog feeling like more of a success than a failure as you begin to test his training in increasingly more distracting and difficult situations.

As he gets the hang of it—he stays until you say "OK"— you can gradually push for longer times—up to a minute on a sit-stay, and up to three minutes on a down-stay. You can also gradually add distractions and work in new environments. To add a minor self-correction for the down-stay, stand on the dog's leash after he lies down, allowing about three inches of slack. If he tries to get up before you've said "OK," he'll discover it doesn't work.

Do not step on the leash to make your dog lie down! This could badly hurt his neck, and will destroy his trust in you. Remember, we are teaching our dogs to make the best choices, not inflicting our answers upon them!

Come

Rather than thinking of "come" as an action—"come to me"—think of it as a place—"the dog is sitting in front of me, facing me." Since your dog by now really likes sitting to earn your touch and other positive reinforcement, he's likely to sometimes sit directly in front of you, facing you, all on his own. When this happens, give it a specific name: "come."

Now follow the rest of the training steps you have learned to make him like doing it and reinforce the behavior by practicing it any chance you get. Anything your dog wants and likes could be earned as a result of his first offering the sit-in-front known as "come."

You can help guide him into the right location. Use your hands as "landing gear" and pat the insides of your legs at his nose level. Do this while backing up a bit, to help him maneuver to the straight-in-front, facing-you position. Don't say the

Pat the insides of your legs to show your dog exactly where you like him to sit when you say "come."

word "come" while he's maneuvering, because he hasn't! You are trying to make "come" the end result, not the work in progress.

You can also help your dog by marking his movement in the right direction: Use your positive sound or word to promise he is getting warm. When he finally sits facing you, enthusiastically say "come," mark again with your positive word, and release him with an enthusiastic "OK!" Make it so worth his while, with lots of play and praise, that he can't wait for you to ask him to come again!

Building a Better Recall

Practice, practice, practice. Now, practice some more. Teach your dog that all good things in life hinge upon him first sitting in front of you in a behavior named "come." When you think he really has got it, test him by asking him to "come" as you gradually add distractions and change locations. Expect setbacks as you make these changes and practice accordingly. Lower your expectations and make his task easier so he is able to get it right. Use those distractions as rewards, when they are appropriate. For example, let him check out the interesting leaf that blew by as a reward for first coming to you and ignoring it.

Add distance and call your dog to come while he is on his retractable leash. If he refuses and sits looking at you blankly, *do not* jerk, tug, "pop," or reel him in. Do nothing! It is his move; wait to see what behavior he offers. He'll either begin to approach (mark the behavior with an excited "good!"), sit and do nothing (just keep waiting), or he'll try to move in some direction other than toward you. If he tries to leave, use your correction marker—"eh!"— and bring him to a stop by letting him walk to the end of the leash, *not* by jerking him. Now walk to him in a neutral manner, and don't jerk or show any disapproval. Gently bring him back to the spot where he was when you called him, then back away and face him, still waiting and not reissuing your command. Let him keep examining his options until he finds the one that works—yours!

If you have practiced everything I've suggested so far and given your dog a chance to really learn what "come" means, he is well aware of what you want and is quite intelligently weighing all his options. The only way he'll know your way is the one that works is to be allowed to examine his other choices and discover that they *don't* work.

Sooner or later every dog tests his training. Don't be offended or angry when your dog tests you. No matter how positive you've made it, he won't always want to do everything you ask, every time. When he explores the "what happens if I don't" scenario, your training is being strengthened. He will discover through his own process of trial and error that the best—and only—way out of a command he really doesn't feel compelled to obey is to obey it.

Let's Go

Many pet owners wonder if they can retain control while walking their dogs and still allow at least some running in front, sniffing, and playing. You might worry that allowing your dog occasional freedom could result in him expecting it all the time, leading to a testy, leash-straining walk. It's possible for both parties on the leash to have an enjoyable experience by implementing and reinforcing well-thought-out training techniques.

Begin by making word associations you'll use on your walks. Give the dog some slack on the leash, and as he starts to walk away from you say "OK" and begin to follow him.

Do not let him drag you; set the pace even when he is being given a turn at being the leader. Whenever he starts to pull, just come to a standstill and refuse to move (or refuse to allow him to continue forward) until there is slack in the leash. Do this correction without saying anything at all. When he isn't pulling, you may decide to just stand still and let him sniff about within the range the slack leash allows, or you may even mosey along following him. After a few minutes of "recess," it is time to work. Say something like "that's it" or "time's up," close the distance between you and your dog, and touch him.

Next say "let's go" (or whatever command you want to use to mean "follow me as we walk"). Turn and walk off, and, if he follows, mark his behavior with "good!" Then stop,

Give your dog slack on his leash as you walk and let him make the decision to walk with you.

When your dog catches up with you, make sure you let him know what a great dog he is!

Intersperse periods of attentive walking, where your dog is on a shorter leash, with periods on a slack leash, where he is allowed to look and sniff around.

squat down, and let him catch you. Make him glad he did! Start again, and do a few transitions as he gets the hang of your follow-the-leader game, speeding up, slowing down, and trying to make it fun. When you stop, he gets to catch up and receive some deserved positive reinforcement. Don't forget that's the reason he is following you, so be sure to make it worth his while!

Require him to remain attentive to you. Do not allow sniffing, playing, eliminating, or pulling during your time as leader on a walk. If he seems to get distracted—which, by the way, is the main reason dogs walk poorly with their people—change direction or pace without saying a word. Just help him realize "oops, I lost track of my human." Do not jerk his neck and say "heel"—this will make the word "heel" mean pain in the neck and will not encourage him to cooperate with you. Don't repeat "let's go," either. He needs to figure out that it is his job to keep track of and follow you if he wants to earn the positive benefits you provide.

The best reward you can give a dog for performing an attentive, controlled walk is a few minutes of walking without all of the controls. Of course, he must remain on a leash even during the "recess" parts of the walk, but allowing him to discriminate between attentive following—"let's go"—and having a few moments of relaxation—"OK"—will increase his willingness to work.

Training for Attention

Your dog pretty much has a one-track mind. Once he is focused on something, everything else is excluded. This can be great, for instance, when he's focusing on you! But it can also be dangerous if, for example, his attention is riveted on the bunny he is chasing and he does not hear you call—that is, not unless he has been trained to pay attention when you say his name.

When you say your dog's name, you'll want him to make eye contact with you. Begin teaching this by making yourself so intriguing that he can't help but look.

When you call your dog's name, you will again be seeking a specific response—eye contact. The best way to teach this is to trigger his alerting response by making a noise with your mouth, such as whistling or a kissing sound, and then immediately doing something he'll find very intriguing.

You can play a treasure hunt game to help teach him to regard his name as a request for attention. As a bonus, you can reinforce the rest of his new vocabulary at the same time.

Treasure Hunt

Make a kissing sound, then jump up and find a dog toy or dramatically raid the fridge and rather noisily eat a piece of cheese. After doing this twice, make a kissing sound and then look at your dog.

Of course he is looking at you! He is waiting to see if that sound—the kissing sound—means you're going to go hunting again. After all, you're so good at it! Because he is looking, say his name, mark with "good," then go hunting and find his toy. Release it to him with an "OK." At any point if he follows you, attach your "let's go!" command; if he leaves you, give permission with "OK."

Using this approach, he cannot be wrong—any behavior your dog offers can be named. You can add things like "take it" when he picks up a toy, and "thank you" when he happens to drop one. Many opportunities to make your new vocabulary meaningful and positive can be found within this simple training game.

Problems to watch out for when teaching the treasure hunt:

- You really do not want your dog to come to you when you call his name (later, when you try to engage his attention to ask him to stay, he'll already be on his way toward you). You just want him to look at you.
- Saying "watch me, watch me" doesn't teach your dog to *offer* his attention. It just makes you a background noise.
- Don't lure your dog's attention with the reward. Get his attention and then reward him for looking. Try holding a toy in one hand with your arm stretched out to your side. Wait until he looks at you rather than the toy. Now say his name then mark with "good!" and release the toy. As he goes for it, say "OK."

To get your dog's attention, try holding his toy with your arm out to your side. Wait until he looks at you, then mark the moment and give him the toy.

Teaching Cooperation

Never punish your dog for failing to obey you or try to punish him into compliance. Bribing, repeating yourself, and doing a behavior for him all avoid the real issue of dog training—his will. He must be helped to be willing, not made to achieve tasks. Good dog training helps your dog want to obey. He learns that he can gain what he values most through cooperation and compliance, and can't gain those things any other way.

Your dog is learning to *earn,* rather than expect, the good things in life. And you've become much more important to him than you were before. Because you are allowing him to experiment and learn, he doesn't have to be forced, manipulated, or bribed. When he wants something, he can gain it by cooperating with you. One of those "somethings"—and a great reward you shouldn't underestimate—is your positive attention, paid to him with love and sincere approval!

Chapter 10

Housetraining Your Bulldog

Excerpted from Housetraining: An Owner's Guide to a Happy Healthy Pet, 1st Edition, *by September Morn*

By the time puppies are about 3 weeks old, they start to follow their mother around. When they are a few steps away from their clean sleeping area, the mama dog stops. The pups try to nurse but mom won't allow it. The pups mill around in frustration, then nature calls and they all urinate and defecate here, away from their bed. The mother dog returns to the nest, with her brood waddling behind her. Their first housetraining lesson has been a success.

The next one to housetrain puppies should be their breeder. The breeder watches as the puppies eliminate, then deftly removes the soiled papers and replaces them with clean papers before the pups can traipse back through their messes. He has wisely arranged the puppies' space so their bed, food, and drinking water are as far away from the elimination area as possible. This way, when the pups follow their mama, they will move away from their sleeping and eating area before eliminating. This habit will help the pups be easily housetrained.

Your Housetraining Shopping List

While your puppy's mother and breeder are getting her started on good house-training habits, you'll need to do some shopping. If you have all the essentials in place before your dog arrives, it will be easier to help her learn the rules from day one.

Newspaper: The younger your puppy and larger her breed, the more newspapers you'll need. Newspaper is absorbent, abundant, cheap, and convenient.

Puddle Pads: If you prefer not to stockpile newspaper, a commercial alternative is puddle pads. These thick paper pads can be purchased under several trade names at pet supply stores. The pads have waterproof backing, so puppy urine doesn't seep through onto the floor. Their disadvantages are that they will cost you more than newspapers and that they contain plastics that are not biodegradable.

Poop Removal Tool: There are several types of poop removal tools available. Some are designed with a separate pan and rake, and others have the handles hinged like scissors. Some scoops need two hands for operation, while others are designed for one-handed use. Try out the different brands at your pet supply store. Put a handful of pebbles or dog kibble on the floor and then pick them up with each type of scoop to determine which works best for you.

Plastic Bags: When you take your dog outside your yard, you *must* pick up after her. Dog waste is unsightly, smelly, and can harbor disease. In many cities and towns, the law mandates dog owners clean up pet waste deposited on public ground. Picking up after your dog using a plastic bag scoop is simple. Just put your hand inside the bag, like a mitten, and then grab the droppings. Turn the bag inside out, tie the top, and that's that.

Crate: To housetrain a puppy, you will need some way to confine her when you're unable to supervise. A dog crate is a secure way to confine your dog for short periods during the day and to use as a comfortable bed at night. Crates come in wire mesh and in plastic. The wire ones are foldable to store flat in a smaller space. The plastic ones are more cozy, draft-free, and quiet, and are approved for airline travel.

Baby Gates: Since you shouldn't crate a dog for more than an hour or two at a time during the day, baby gates are a good way to limit your dog's freedom in the house. Be sure the baby gates you use are safe. The old-fashioned wooden, expanding lattice type has seriously injured a number of children by collapsing and trapping a leg, arm, or neck. That type of gate can hurt a puppy, too, so use the modern grid type gates instead. You'll need more than one baby gate if you have several doorways to close off.

Exercise Pen: Portable exercise pens are great when you have a young pup or a small dog. These metal or plastic pens are made of rectangular panels that are hinged together. The pens are freestanding, sturdy, foldable, and can be carried like a suitcase. You could set one up in your kitchen as the pup's daytime corral, and then take it outdoors to contain your pup while you garden or just sit and enjoy the day.

Enzymatic Cleaner: All dogs make housetraining mistakes. Accept this and be ready for it by buying an enzymatic cleaner made especially for pet accidents. Dogs like to eliminate where they have done it before, and lingering smells lead them to those spots. Ordinary household cleaners may remove all the odors you can smell, but only an enzymatic cleaner will remove everything your dog can smell.

The First Day

Housetraining is a matter of establishing good habits in your dog. That means you never want her to learn anything she will eventually have to unlearn. Start off housetraining on the right foot by teaching your dog that you prefer her to eliminate outside. Designate a potty area in your backyard (if you have one) or in the street in front of your home and take your dog to it as soon as you arrive home. Let her sniff a bit and, when she squats to go, give the action a name: "potty" or "do it" or anything else you won't be embarrassed to say in public. Eventually your dog will associate that word with the act and will eliminate on command. When she's finished, praise her with "good potty!"

That first day, take your puppy out to the potty area frequently. Although she may not eliminate every time, you are establishing a routine: You take her to her spot, ask her to eliminate, and praise her when she does.

Just before bedtime, take your dog to her potty area once more. Stand by and wait until she produces. Do not put your dog to bed for the night until she has eliminated. Be patient and calm. This is not the time to play with or excite your

Take your pup out frequently to her special potty spot and praise her when she goes.

dog. If she's too excited, a pup not only won't eliminate, she probably won't want to sleep either.

Most dogs, even young ones, will not soil their beds if they can avoid it. For this reason, a sleeping crate can be a tremendous help during housetraining. Being crated at night can help a dog develop the muscles that control elimination. So after your dog has emptied out, put her to bed in her crate.

A good place to put your dog's sleeping crate is near your own bed. Dogs are pack animals, so they feel safer sleeping with others in a common area. In your bedroom, the pup will be near you and you'll be close enough to hear when she wakes during the night and needs to eliminate.

> ### TIP
>
> #### Water
>
> Make sure your dog has access to clean water at all times. Limiting the amount of water a dog drinks is not necessary for housetraining success and can be very dangerous. A dog needs water to digest food, to maintain a proper body temperature and proper blood volume, and to clean her system of toxins and wastes. A healthy dog will automatically drink the right amount. Do not restrict water intake. Controlling your dog's access to water is not the key to housetraining her; controlling her access to everything else in your home is.

> ## Don't Overuse the Crate
>
> A crate serves well as a dog's overnight bed, but you should not leave the dog in her crate for more than an hour or two during the day. Throughout the day, she needs to play and exercise. She is likely to want to drink some water and will undoubtedly eliminate. Confining your dog all day will give her no option but to soil her crate. This is not just unpleasant for you and the dog, but it reinforces bad cleanliness habits. And crating a pup for the whole day is abusive. Don't do it.

Pups under 4 months old often are not able to hold their urine all night. If your puppy has settled down to sleep but awakens and fusses a few hours later, she probably needs to go out. For the best housetraining progress, take your pup to her elimination area whenever she needs to go, even in the wee hours of the morning.

Your pup may soil in her crate if you ignore her late night urgency. It's unfair to let this happen, and it sends the wrong message about your expectations for cleanliness. Resign yourself to this midnight outing and just get up and take the pup out. Your pup will outgrow this need soon and will learn in the process that she can count on you, and you'll wake happily each morning to a clean dog.

The next morning, the very first order of business is to take your pup out to eliminate. Don't forget to take her to her special potty spot, ask her to eliminate, and then praise her when she does. After your pup empties out in the morning, give her breakfast, and then take her to her potty area again. After that, she shouldn't need to eliminate again right away, so you can allow her some free playtime. Keep an eye on the pup though, because when she pauses in play, she may need to go potty. Take her to the right spot, give the command, and praise if she produces.

Confine Your Pup

A pup or dog who has not finished housetraining should *never* be allowed the run of the house unattended. A new dog (especially a puppy) with unlimited access to your house will make her own choices about where to eliminate.

Vigilance during your new dog's first few weeks in your home will pay big dividends. Every potty mistake delays housetraining progress; every success speeds it along.

Prevent problems by setting up a controlled environment for your new pet. A good place for a puppy corral is often the kitchen. Kitchens almost always have waterproof or easily cleaned floors, which is a distinct asset with leaky pups. A bathroom, laundry room, or enclosed porch could be used for a puppy corral, but the kitchen is generally the best location. Kitchens are a meeting place and a hub of activity for many families, and a puppy will learn better manners when she is socialized thoroughly with family, friends, and nice strangers.

Your dog's crate is a great housetraining tool.

The way you structure your pup's corral area is very important. Her bed, food, and water should be at the opposite end of the corral from the potty area. When you first get your pup, spread newspaper over the rest of the floor of her playpen corral. Lay the papers at least four pages thick and be sure to overlap the edges. As you note the pup's progress, you can remove the papers nearest the sleeping and eating corner. Gradually decrease the size of the papered area until only the end where you want the pup to eliminate is covered. If you will be training your dog to eliminate outside, place newspaper at the end of the corral that is closest to the door that leads outdoors. That way as she moves away from the clean area to the papered area, the pup will also form the habit of heading toward the door to go out.

Maintain a scent marker for the pup's potty area by reserving a small soiled piece of paper when you clean up. Place this piece, with her scent of urine, under the top sheet of the clean papers you spread. This will cue your pup where to eliminate.

Most dog owners use a combination of indoor papers and outdoor elimination areas. When the pup is left by herself in the corral, she can potty on the ever-present newspaper. When you are available to take the pup outside, she can do her business in the outdoor spot. It is not difficult to switch a pup from

Start your pup with a big area of paper to pee on; eventually, you can make it smaller.

indoor paper training to outdoor elimination. Owners of large pups often switch early, but potty papers are still useful if the pup spends time in her indoor corral while you're away. Use the papers as long as your pup needs them. If you come home and they haven't been soiled, you are ahead.

When setting up your pup's outdoor yard, put the lounging area as far away as possible from the potty area, just as with the indoor corral setup. People with large yards, for example, might leave a patch unmowed at the edge of the lawn to serve as the dog's elimination area. Other dog owners teach the dog to relieve herself in a designated corner of a deck or patio. For an apartment-dwelling city dog, the outdoor potty area might be a tiny balcony or the curb. Each dog owner has somewhat different expectations for their dog. Teach your dog to eliminate in a spot that suits your environment and lifestyle.

Be sure to pick up droppings in your yard at least once a day. Dogs have a natural desire to stay far away from their own excrement, and if too many piles litter the ground, your dog won't want to walk through it and will start eliminating elsewhere. Leave just one small piece of feces in the potty area to remind your dog where the right spot is located.

To help a pup adapt to the change from indoors to outdoors, take one of her potty papers outside to the new elimination area. Let the pup stand on the paper when she goes potty outdoors. Each day for four days, reduce the size of the paper by half. By the fifth day, the pup, having used a smaller and smaller piece of paper to stand on, will probably just go to that spot and eliminate.

Take your pup to her outdoor potty place frequently throughout the day. A puppy can hold her urine for only about as many hours as her age in months, and will move her bowels as many times a day as she eats. So a 2-month-old pup will urinate about every two hours, while at 4 months she can manage about four hours between piddles. Pups vary somewhat in their rate of development, so this is not a hard and fast rule. It does, however, present a realistic idea of how long a pup can be left without access to a potty place. Past 4 months, her potty trips will be less frequent.

Take your dog out frequently for regularly scheduled walks.

When you take the dog outdoors to her spot, keep her leashed so that she won't wander away. Stand quietly and let her sniff around in the designated area. If your pup starts to leave before she has eliminated, gently lead her back and remind her to go. If your pup sniffs at the spot, praise her calmly, say the command word, and just wait. If she produces, praise serenely, then give her time to sniff around a little more. She may not be finished, so give her time to go again before allowing her to play and explore her new home.

If you find yourself waiting more than five minutes for your dog to potty, take her back inside. Watch your pup carefully for twenty minutes, not giving her any opportunity to slip away to eliminate unnoticed. If you are too busy to watch the pup, put her in her crate. After twenty minutes, take her to the outdoor potty spot again and tell her what to do. If you're unsuccessful after five minutes, crate the dog again. Give her another chance to eliminate in fifteen or twenty minutes. Eventually, she will have to go.

Watch Your Pup

Be vigilant and don't let the pup make a mistake in the house. Each time you successfully anticipate elimination and take your pup to the potty spot, you'll move a step closer to your goal. Stay aware of your puppy's needs. If you ignore the pup, she will make mistakes and you'll be cleaning up more messes.

Keep a chart of your new dog's elimination behavior for the first three or four days. Jot down what times she eats, sleeps, and eliminates. After several days a pattern will emerge that can help you determine your pup's body rhythms. Most dogs tend to eliminate at fairly regular intervals. Once you know your new dog's natural rhythms, you'll be able to anticipate her needs and schedule appropriate potty outings.

Understanding the meanings of your dog's postures can also help you win the battle of the puddle. When your dog is getting ready to eliminate, she will display a specific set of postures. The sooner you can learn to read these signals, the cleaner your floor will stay.

A young puppy who feels the urge to eliminate may start to sniff the ground and walk in a circle. If the pup is very young, she may simply squat and go. All young puppies, male or female, squat to urinate. If you are housetraining a pup under 4 months of age, regardless of sex, watch for the beginnings of a squat as the signal to rush the pup to the potty area.

When a puppy is getting ready to defecate, she may run urgently back and forth or turn in a circle while sniffing or starting to squat. If defecation is imminent, the pup's anus may protrude or open slightly. When she starts to go, the pup will squat and hunch her back, her tail sticking straight out behind. There is no mistaking this posture; nothing else looks like this. If your pup takes this position, take her to her potty area. Hurry! You may have to carry her to get there in time.

A young puppy won't have much time between feeling the urge and actually eliminating, so you'll have to be quick to note her postural clues and intercept your pup in time. Pups from 3 to 6 months have a few seconds more between the urge and the act than younger ones do. The older your pup, the more time you'll have to get her to the potty area after she begins the posture signals that alert you to her need.

Accidents Happen

If you see your pup about to eliminate somewhere other than the designated area, interrupt her immediately. Say "wait, wait, wait!" or clap your hands loudly to startle her into stopping. Carry the pup, if she's still small enough, or take her collar and lead her to the correct area. Once your dog is in the potty area, give her the command to eliminate. Use a friendly voice for the command, then wait patiently for her to produce. The pup may be tense because you've just startled her and may have to relax a bit before she's able to eliminate. When she does her job, include the command word in the praise you give ("good potty").

The old-fashioned way of housetraining involved punishing a dog's mistakes even before she knew what she was supposed to do. Puppies were punished for breaking rules they didn't understand about functions they couldn't control.

It's not fair to expect your baby puppy to be able to control herself the way an adult dog can.

This was not fair. While your dog is new to housetraining, there is no need or excuse for punishing her mistakes. Your job is to take the dog to the potty area just before she needs to go, especially with pups under 3 months old. If you aren't watching your pup closely enough and she has an accident, don't punish the puppy for your failure to anticipate her needs. It's not the pup's fault; it's yours.

In any case, punishment is not an effective tool for housetraining most dogs. Many will react to punishment by hiding puddles and feces where you won't find them right away (like behind the couch or under the desk). This eventually may lead to punishment after the fact, which leads to more hiding, and so on.

Instead of punishing for mistakes, stay a step ahead of potty accidents by learning to anticipate your pup's needs. Accompany your dog to the designated potty area when she needs to go. Tell her what you want her to do and praise her when she goes. This will work wonders. Punishment won't be necessary if you are a good teacher.

What happens if you come upon a mess after the fact? Some trainers say a dog can't remember having eliminated, even a few moments after she has done so. This is not true. The fact is that urine and feces carry a dog's unique scent, which she (and every other dog) can instantly recognize. So, if you happen upon a potty mistake after the fact you can still use it to teach your dog.

But remember, no punishment! Spanking, hitting, shaking, or scaring a puppy for having a housetraining accident is confusing and counterproductive. Spend your energy instead on positive forms of teaching.

Take your pup and a paper towel to the mess. Point to the urine or feces and calmly tell your puppy, "no potty here." Then scoop or sop up the accident with the paper towel. Take the evidence and the pup to the approved potty area. Drop the mess on the ground and tell the dog, "good potty here," as if she had done the deed in the right place. If your pup sniffs at the evidence, praise her calmly. If the accident happened very recently, your dog may not have to go yet, but wait with her a few minutes anyway. If she eliminates, praise her. Afterwards, go finish cleaning up the mess.

Soon the puppy will understand that there is a place where you are pleased about elimination and other places where you are not. Praising for elimination in the approved place will help your pup remember the rules.

Scheduling Basics

With a new puppy in the home, don't be surprised if your rising time is suddenly a little earlier than you've been accustomed to. Puppies have earned a reputation as very early risers. When your pup wakes you at the crack of dawn, you will have to get up and take her to her elimination spot. Be patient. When your dog is an adult, she may enjoy sleeping in as much as you do.

At the end of the chapter, you'll find typical housetraining schedules for puppies under 10 weeks, puppies aged 10 weeks to 6 months, and adolescent and adult dogs. It's fine to adjust the rising times when using the schedule for puppies under 10 weeks, but you should not adjust the intervals between feedings and potty outings unless your pup's behavior justifies a change. Your puppy can only meet your expectations in housetraining if you help her learn the rules.

Housetraining is a huge task, but it doesn't go on forever. Be patient and soon your dog will be reliable.

The schedule for puppies is devised with the assumption that someone will be home most of the time with the pup. That would be the best scenario, of course, but is not always possible. You may be able to ease the problems of a latchkey pup by having a neighbor or friend look in on the pup at noon and take her to eliminate. A better solution might be hiring a pet sitter to drop by midday. A professional pet sitter will be knowledgeable about companion animals and can give your pup high-quality care and socialization. Some can even help train your pup in both potty manners and basic obedience. Ask your veterinarian and your dog-owning friends to recommend a good pet sitter.

If you must leave your pup alone during her early housetraining period, be sure to cover the entire floor of her corral with thick layers of overlapping newspaper. If you come home to messes in the puppy corral, just clean them up. Be patient—she's still a baby.

Use the schedules here as a basic plan to help prevent housetraining accidents. Meanwhile, use your own powers of observation to discover how to best modify the basic schedule to fit your dog's unique needs. Each dog is an individual and will have her own rhythms, and each dog is reliable at a different age.

Schedule for Pups Under 10 Weeks

11 p.m.	Lay out easy-on clothes and shoes before going to bed. There will be no time to choose your wardrobe in the morning when you jump out of bed to take your pup to her potty place. And don't forget your house keys!
7:00 a.m.	Get up and take the puppy from her sleeping crate directly to the potty spot. Carry her if necessary.
7:15	Clean up last night's messes, if any.
7:30	Food and fresh water.
7:45	Pick up the food bowl. Take the pup to her potty spot; wait and praise.
8:00	The pup plays around your feet while you drink coffee and prepare breakfast. It has now been one hour since you got up. Console yourself that, if you've been following this schedule so far, you shouldn't have had any new messes to clean up for the past hour.

continues

Schedule for Pups Under 10 Weeks (continued)

8:15	Potty time again.
8:30	Put the pup in her crate for a nap.
10:00	When the pup wakes, out to potty.
10:15	The puppy is in her corral with safe toys to chew and play with. As you watch your pup at play, observe her behavior. Learn to recognize what she does immediately before eliminating. Any sudden searching, sniffing, or circling behavior is a likely sign she has to go. As soon as you see that, carry or lead the pup to her potty spot and calmly tell her to eliminate. Praise her success. If you miss the moment and arrive sometime after the flood, do not scold or punish. It's not the pup's fault you were late.
10:45	Potty break.
11:00	Playtime.
11:30	Potty time again.
11:45	Food and fresh water.
12:00 p.m.	Pick up the food bowl and take the pup to her potty spot.
12:15	Crate the pup for a nap with a safe chew toy.
2:00	Potty break.
2:15	Snack and beginner obedience training practice.
2:45	Potty break.
3:00	Put the pup in her corral with safe toys and chews for solitary play and/or a nap.
4:15	Potty break.
4:30	Make the pup a part of household activities by putting her on a leash and taking her around the house with you. Watch and guide your pup's behavior. When she needs to eliminate, you'll be right there to notice, take her to the right spot in time, and praise her good job.

5:00	Food and fresh water.
5:15	Potty break.
5:30	The pup may play nearby (either leashed or in her corral) while you prepare your evening meal.
6:00	Potty break, then crate the pup while you eat and clean up after dinner.
7:00	Potty break.
7:15	Leashed or closely watched, this is a good time for the pup to play and socialize with family and visitors for a few hours. Offer the pup water occasionally throughout the evening (a dog needs water to digest her food). Take the pup to the potty spot whenever she acts like she needs to go.
9:00	Last water of the evening.
9:15	Potty break. Then crate pup or keep her close to you. Do not let her wander off unescorted.
10:45	Last chance to potty.
11:00	Put the pup to bed in her crate for the night. Go to bed yourself and get some rest. You've earned it!
3:00 or 4:00 a.m.	Your pup awakes and has to eliminate. Take her to the potty spot and make sure she does everything she has to do. Then re-crate the pup with a safe, quiet chew toy and go back to sleep.

You'll notice that this schedule calls for you to take your pup to the potty area about fifteen times a day. That may be more than your pup needs, but you should take her that often at first. After keeping track for a few days, you'll start to notice your pup's own digestion and elimination body rhythms. As you learn your pup's needs, you can adjust the schedule to meet them.

Schedule for Pups 10 Weeks to 6 Months

7:00 a.m.	Get up and take the puppy from her sleeping crate to her potty spot.
7:15	Clean up last night's messes, if any.
7:30	Food and fresh water.
7:45	Pick up the food bowl. Take the pup to her potty spot; wait and praise.
8:00	The pup plays around your feet while you have your breakfast.
9:00	Potty break (younger pups may not be able to wait this long).
9:15	Play and obedience practice.
10:00	Potty break.
10:15	The puppy is in her corral with safe toys to chew and play with.
11:30	Potty break (younger pups may not be able to wait this long).
11:45	Food and fresh water.
12:00 p.m.	Pick up the food bowl and take the pup to her potty spot.
12:15	The puppy is in her corral with safe toys to chew and play with.
1:00	Potty break (younger pups may not be able to wait this long).
1:15	Put the pup on a leash and take her around the house with you.
3:30	Potty break (younger pups may not be able to wait this long).
3:45	Put the pup in her corral with safe toys and chews for solitary play and/or a nap.
4:45	Potty break.
5:00	Food and fresh water.
5:15	Potty break.

5:30	The pup may play nearby (either leashed or in her corral) while you prepare your evening meal.
7:00	Potty break.
7:15	Leashed or closely watched, the pup may play and socialize with family and visitors.
9:15	Potty break (younger pups may not be able to wait this long).
10:45	Last chance to potty.
11:00	Put the pup to bed in her crate for the night.

Schedule for Adolescent and Adult Dogs

7:00 a.m.	Get up and take the dog from her sleeping crate directly to the potty spot.
7:30	Food and fresh water.
7:45	Pick up the food bowl and take dog to her potty spot.
8:00	Allow dog to play or lounge with you. Provide chew toys.
10:00	Potty break.
10:15	Play and obedience practice.
11:45	Potty break.
12:00 p.m.	Food and fresh water.
12:15	Pick up the food bowl and take dog to her potty spot.
12:45	Solitary play in the room with you or outdoors in a fenced yard.
2:45	Potty break.
3:00	Put the dog on a leash and take her around the house with you; or, if she is reliably housetrained, this can be free time.
5:00	Food and fresh water.

continues

Schedule for Adolescent and Adult Dogs *(continued)*

5:15	Pick up the food bowl and take dog to her potty spot.
5:30	Keep the dog with you while you prepare and eat your meal.
7:15	Potty break.
7:30	Closely watched, the dog plays off leash and socializes with the family.
9:30	Potty break.
10:45	Last chance to potty.
11:00	Crate the dog for the night.

Appendix

Learning More about Your Bulldog

Some Good Books

About Bulldogs

Ewing, Susan. *Bulldogs For Dummies*. John Wiley and Sons, 2006.
Gagne, Tammy. *Bulldogs*. TFH Publications, 2007.
Morgan, Diane, with Wayne Hunthausen, DVM. *The Bulldog*. TFH Publications, 2005.
Thomas, Chris. *Bulldogs Today*. Ringpress Books, 2000.

About Health Care

Arden, Darlene. *The Angell Memorial Animal Hospital Book of Wellness and Preventive Care for Dogs*. Contemporary Books, 2003.
Eldredge, Debra, DVM, and Delbert Carlson, DVM, Liisa Carlson, DVM, James Giffin, MD. *Dog Owner's Home Veterinary Handbook*, 4th edition. Howell Book House, 2007.
Goldstein, Robert S., VMD, and Susan J. Goldstein. *The Goldsteins' Wellness and Longevity Program*. TFH Publications, 2005.
Messonnier, Shawn, DVM. *Eight Weeks to a Healthy Dog*. Rodale Books, 2003.

About Training

McCullough, Susan. *Housetraining For Dummies.* John Wiley and Sons, 2002.
Palika, Liz. *All Dogs Need Some Training.* Howell Book House, 1997.
Palika, Liz. *The KISS Guide to Raising a Puppy.* Dorling Kindersley, 2002.
Smith, Cheryl. *The Rosetta Bone.* Howell Book House, 2004.

Dog Sports and Activities

Davis, Kathy Diamond. *Therapy Dogs.* Howell Book House, 1992.
Owens Wright, Sue. *150 Activities for Bored Dogs: Sure-fire Ways to Keep Your Dog Active and Happy.* Adams Media, 2007.
Palika, Liz. *The Complete Idiot's Guide to Dog Tricks.* Alpha Books, 2005.

Magazines

AKC Gazette
260 Madison Ave.
New York, NY 10016
www.akc.org/pubs/index.cfm

Bloodlines
100 East Kilgore Rd.
Kalamazoo, MI 49002
www.ukcdogs.com

The Bulldogger
4300 Town Road
Salem, WI 53168
www.thebca.org/bulldogger.html

Dog Fancy
P.O. Box 37185
Boone, IA 50037-0185
www.dogfancy.com

Dog World
P.O. Box 37185
Boone, IA 50037-0185
www.dogworldmag.com

Clubs and Registries

The Bulldog Club of America
Secretary: Kathy Moss
mossrose@ev1.net
www.thebca.org

This is the national club for the breed; its Web site has a great deal of information, including upcoming shows and competitions. There are also many all-breed, individual breed, canine sport, and other special-interest dog clubs across the country. The registries listed below can help you find clubs in your area.

American Kennel Club
260 Madison Ave.
New York, NY 10016
(212) 696-8200
www.akc.org

Canadian Kennel Club
200 Ronson Dr.
Etobicoke, Ontario
Canada M9W 5Z9
(800) 250-8040 or (416) 675-5511
www.ckc.ca

United Kennel Club
100 East Kilgore Rd.
Kalamazoo, MI 49002
(616) 343-9020
www.ukcdogs.com

On the Internet

All About Bulldogs

Bulldog Breeds.com
www.bulldogbreeds.com
Dedicated to all of the bully breeds, including English Bulldogs, with breed information, breeders, photos, and forums.

The Bulldog Club of America Rescue Network
www.rescuebulldogs.org
This site has information about Bulldogs, how the rescue organization works, adoption policies, and much more.

Bulldog Domain
www.bulldogdomain.com
All about Bulldogs, including rescue, feeding, safety, health concerns, and more.

The Bulldog Information Library
www.bulldoginformation.com
You'll find extensive information on Bulldog history, art, care, showing, toys, and even Bulldog humor.

Bullwrinkle Bulldog Health & Care Topics
www.bullwrinkle.com/Bulldog%20Health.htm
This is a glossary of health and care subjects focused on Bulldogs. This includes many common medications as well as diseases and health problems.

The English Bulldog
www.bulldoginformation.com
The English Bulldog Information Library with articles about Bulldog health, care, breeding, and more. Lots of Bulldog photos.

Canine Health

American Veterinary Medical Association
www.avma.org
The American Veterinary Medical Association Web site has a wealth of information for dog owners, from disaster preparedness to both common and rare diseases affecting canines. There is also information on choosing the right dog and dog bite prevention.

Canine Health Information Center
www.caninehealthinfo.org
The Canine Health Information Center is a centralized canine health database jointly sponsored by the American Kennel Club Canine Health Foundation and the Orthopedic Foundation for Animals.

Dog Sports and Activities

Dog Patch
www.dogpatch.org
Information on many different dog sports and activities, including herding, agility, and Frisbee.

Dog Play
www.dog-play.com
More about dog sports and activities, including hiking, backpacking, therapy dog work, and much more.

Photo Credits:
Isabelle Francais: 4, 8–9, 11, 14, 23, 25, 27, 29, 32, 35, 39, 55, 63, 74, 75, 76, 84, 124
Howell Book House: 10
JeanMFogle.com: 1, 21, 24, 40, 44, 45, 48, 53, 58, 59, 61, 64, 66, 69, 81, 88, 89, 95, 96–97, 98, 123, 128
Bonnie Nance: 19, 31, 34, 42, 68, 91 (bottom)
Tammy Raabe Rao/rubicat.com: 13, 16, 18, 20, 26, 30, 38, 49, 50–51, 52, 60, 71, 72, 80, 87, 91 (top), 118, 121, 125, 127

Index